Lincolnshire Almshouses

Nine Centuries of Charitable Housing

by

Linda Crust

with a contribution by Paula Judson

At Quincey's moat the squandering village ends,
And there in the almshouse dwell the dearest friends
Of all the village, two old dames that cling
As close as turtle doves in the spring.
Long, long ago they passed threescore-and-ten,
And in this dolls' house lived together then;
All things they have in common being so poor
And their one fear, Death's shadow at the door.

('Almswomen' by Edmund Blunden, written in the 1920s)

HERITAGE LINCOLNSHIRE

In partnership with
Lincolnshire County Council

First published in the United Kingdom in 2002 by:
Heritage Lincolnshire
The Old School, Cameron Street, Heckington, Sleaford
Lincolnshire, NG34 9RW
A Registered Charity

British Library Cataloguing-in-Publication Data.
A CIP catalogue record for this book
is available from the British Library

ISBN 0-948639-38-5

The historical sources quoted in this book contain many references to pre-decimal British currency. The currency changed to the present decimal system in 1971. The pre-decimal coinage used pounds, shillings and pence (£.s.d.). There were twenty shillings in one pound and twelve pence in one shilling. Amounts may be written as pence (8½d), shillings (3/-), shillings and pence (4/8d or 4s. 8d) or pounds, shillings and pence (£30. 13s. 4d). One shilling is the equivalent of 5 (new) pence.

Designed by Susan Unsworth

Printed in the UK by G W Belton Ltd, Gainsborough

The Heritage Trust of Lincolnshire works in partnership
with Lincolnshire County Council

Front cover photograph:The Henry Godson Almshouses on Heckington village green

Back cover photograph: The Bedehouse at Belton

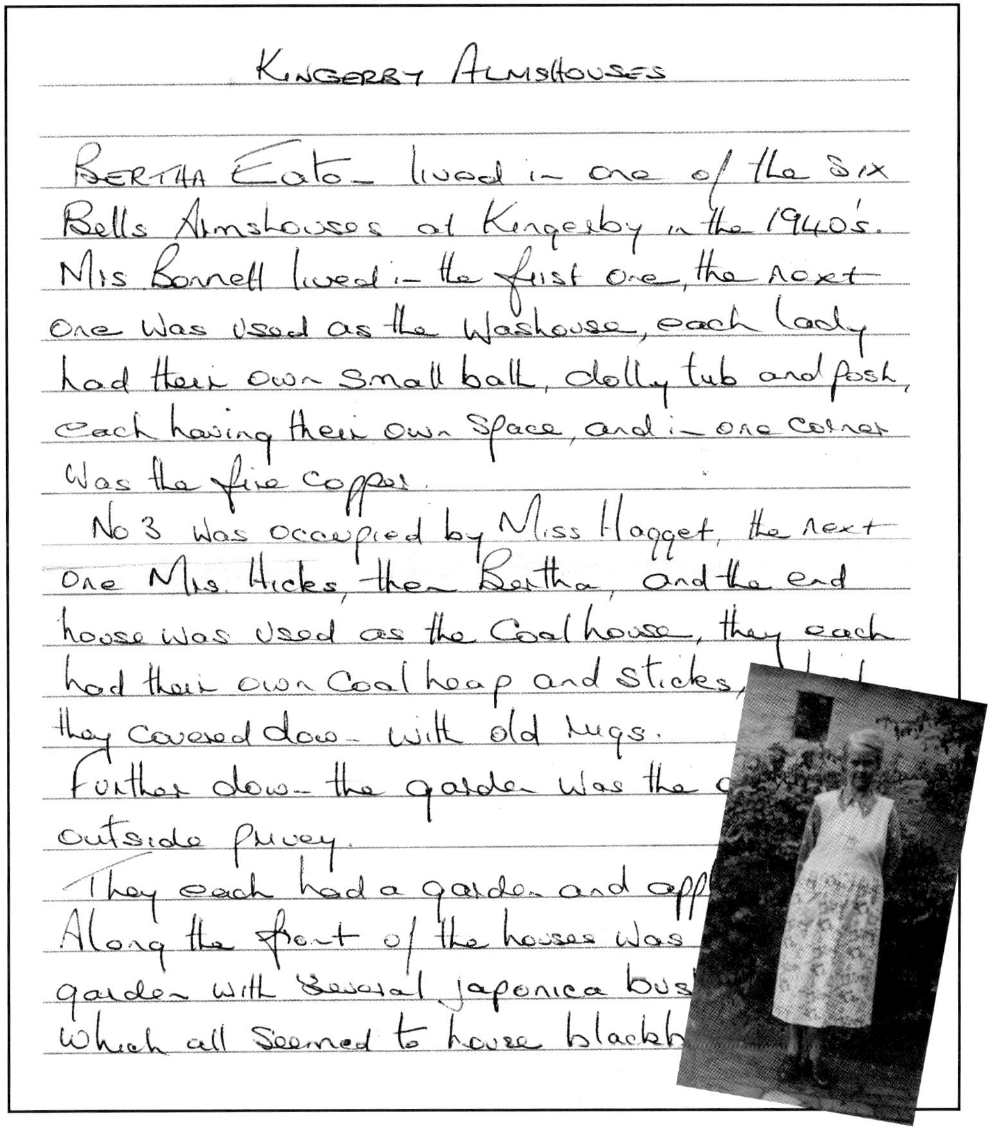
Kingerby Almshouses

Bertha Eaton lived in one of the six Bells Almshouses at Kingerby in the 1940's. Mrs Bonnell lived in the first one, the next one was used as the Washhouse, each lady had their own small bath, dolly tub and posh, each having their own space, and in one corner was the fire copper.
No 3 was occupied by Miss Hogget, the next one Mrs. Hicks, then Bertha, and the end house was used as the Coal house, they each had their own Coal heap and sticks, ...
they covered down with old rugs.
Further down the garden was the ...
outside privey.
They each had a garden and app...
Along the front of the houses was ...
garden with several japonica bus...
which all seemed to house blackb...

Information for this book came from a wide range of sources, many of them personal accounts and recollections. Freda Styles sent the above account of Kingerby Almshouse, together with a photograph of Bertha Eaton, one of the last inhabitants of the building before it was renovated in 1994/95.

CONTENTS

Foreword

Almshouses are amongst the most distinctive and most loved buildings of our towns and villages yet they have received surprisingly little attention from architectural and social historians, whether national or local. In this pioneer work Linda Crust admirably demonstrates what can be done with enthusiasm and determination to record and illustrate this important part of our heritage. She has identified almost 200 foundations commencing with the medieval hospital of the Holy Innocents at Lincoln. Her researches are detailed in the gazetteers which accompany the illuminating accounts of Lincolnshire almshouses in three periods from 1100. Here we learn of centuries of charitable giving as well as of the scandals of mismanagement familiar from the writings of Anthony Trollope, and the seemingly greater philanthropy of the townspeople of Stamford and Spalding than elsewhere in the county.

Lincolnshire can be proud of its past residents who have given the county such a wealth of fine almshouses whose form and architectural style is examined in a chapter by Paula Judson. They range from the outstanding medieval Hospital of All Saints (Browne's), Stamford, through delightful single-storey early seventeenth century brick rows at Tattershall and Fosdyke, ambitious Victorian foundations at Lincoln and Louth, to the eccentric Teetotal Houses at Ruskington and the charming vernacular revival Memorial Cottages at Aylesby, built 1925. There have been losses in recent years, including the tragic destruction of the splendid Welby Almshouses at Denton. Some older almshouses have been sold and replaced by modern housing and others, such as those at Revesby, have been rebuilt in their original form. Fortunately many almshouses have been modernised without altering their external character.

Almshouses are one of those elements of our heritage that are still as relevant today as when first established. With an increasing proportion of the population living on into a long and active retirement the need for suitable accommodation, such as that provided by almshouses, is more important than ever. All around Britain almshouse charities, often with the help of the Almshouse Association, are restoring and updating their historic properties. Unlike many of our historic buildings almshouses, when sympathetically modernised, can still perform the function they were built for. Fortunate is the Lincolnshire town or village that produced a generous donor in the past, whose benefaction not only contributes to the welfare of the community in the twenty-first century but also, as this book shows, adds so pleasurably to our built heritage.

Having attended a school in the shadow of the handsome Handcock's Hospital at Bardney and been a regular visitor to St Anne's Bedehouses at Lincoln, where my mother, two aunts and a cousin were onetime residents, it has given me great pleasure to write the foreword to this excellent publication. Linda Crust has done a great service in chronicling so fully this aspect of Lincolnshire, past and present.

David Neave
Department of History, University of Hull

Acknowledgements

My interest in almshouses started as a passing curiosity and became a passion. I knew the location of perhaps a dozen groups of these houses in the county and thought it would be interesting to find out more about them. To date the learning journey has taken nearly four years and thousands of miles. The variety of foundations, building styles and administration procedures has delighted and amazed me. From medieval hospitals to modern bungalows the story of almshouses is the story of people, their riches, poverty, vicissitudes, triumphs, health, religion and, above all, their housing. I have been privy to a world of welfare through the centuries. I have pestered vicars, trustees, descendants of founders and residents - not to mention librarians, archivists and any member of the public who had relevant or irrelevant information. I thank them all.

In particular my editor, David Start, has matched my enthusiasm, encouraged me and pushed me gently onwards. Without him I would still be floundering in an unfathomable sea of information. As it is, I doubt if the subject will ever be bottomed out, but a line has been drawn and the results are in this book.

My thanks go to David and also to the following: Rex Russell; Dennis Mills; Jean Howard; David Robinson; Brenda Webster; John Taylor; R M Aitken; Richard Lucas; Rick and Sylvia Poulson; Clifford Dack; Paula Judson; Susan Unsworth; Neil Wright; David Markham; Mark Bennet; Gillian Loft; Pat Pomeroy; Susan Edlington; Dennis Peall; Ringrose Law Group; Hilary Healey; Bridget Robinson; David Hopkins; Plus numberless trustees, parish clerks, vicars, almshouse residents and passers-by, and friends and relations for their encouragement and patience.

Any mistakes and omissions are mine.

1100-1550 : Medieval Hospitals "Peculation And Jobbery!"

Almshouses have existed for about 1000 years, the earliest being founded originally as medieval hospitals. The Synod of Aix in 816, which was the cornerstone of monasticism, detailed the distribution of alms as one of the seven Corporal Works of Mercy. At that date infirmaries (farmeries) and hospitals catered for the needs of members of monastic orders or laymen attached to the monasteries. Alms were distributed to poor people to aid them outside the religious houses but no shelter was offered to them. By the twelfth and thirteen centuries the monastic infirmaries were beginning to cater for poor aged and infirm laymen in specially built accommodation. These buildings were known as hospitals. It is from these hospitals that the almshouse, bedehouse, or callis, developed over the centuries. Some hospitals were used as staging posts by pilgrims and other travellers, thus serving the dual purpose of offering shelter and generating income. The term bedehouse or beadhouse (housing bedesmen and bedeswomen) derives from the Middle English term for prayer (*bede*). Indeed, the small, perforated balls that we call beads owe this name to their use for counting prayers. In the term bedehouse, the implication is that residents have a duty to pray for the benefactor.

One definition of a medieval hospital[1] is 'a group of buildings which housed a religious or secular institution which provided spiritual and (limited) bodily care.' Hospitals may be traced from documents (e.g. records of Bishop's visitations), cartographic sources, standing buildings and archaeological remains. The word *hospital* should not be confused with the modern concept of a hospital; its origin is the Latin *hospites* meaning guests. The four main types of medieval hospital are:

a) leper houses
b) almshouses
c) *Maisons Dieu* or guest houses for wayfarers and pilgrims; they were sometimes called *Domus Dei*
d) institutions for the poor and sick.

The unusual term 'Callis', referring to an almshouse, is preserved in this street name in Stamford (Fryer's Callis - No. 178 in the gazetteer). The use of the term Callis may be unique to Stamford for in Joseph Wright's Dialect Dictionary (1898) he notes "The wool of the staple of Calais was of great importance in Stamford and is the origin of the curious local name of Callis for almshouse ... these having been freely built for decayed members of the Staple".

A large hospital would include an infirmary hall, or group of cells, chapel, cemetery, dormitory and refectory, kitchen and garderobe. A water source was obviously necessary. Rawcliffe says that even the meanest medieval hospital buildings would have been decorated with Christian iconography. Images of *Christus Medicus* (Christ the Physician) were popular. Hospitals with a religious foundation (*locus religiosus*), which includes the majority of medieval hospitals in Lincolnshire, had building plans similar to priories. These hospitals such as the Hospital of the Holy Innocents, Lincoln, and the Hospital of Mary Magdalene, Partney, were subject to episcopal visitation and exemption from tithes. Parochial provision such as burial and the right for confession to be heard might be provided. Such religious foundations were usually suppressed at the Reformation although odd ones survived such as that at Spital in the Street and at Mere (parish of Dunston). Many had already disappeared before the sixteenth century. Just outside the county in Lyddington, Rutland, there survives an example of a medieval bedehouse that has been preserved and can be visited. This example exists as a result of the Reformation in that it was formerly part of a palace of the Bishops of Lincoln which was sequestered by the Crown in 1547. Later Sir Thomas Cecil converted the surviving buildings into Jesus Hospital which later became known as the Bede House. It ceased to exist as such in 1930.

Most early hospitals were religious foundations. They could have been founded by royalty (patients of Lincoln Holy Innocents had to have permission of the king to enter); by ecclesiastical sources such as Partney which was a cell of Bardney Abbey; by corporations (Edward VI's of Louth had formerly belonged to St Mary's Guild but was re-founded later) or by secular individuals (St John the Baptist

Lyddington Bede House, Rutland, is an English Heritage property, open to the public (Mar – Oct). Originally built as a Bishops' Palace, it was converted to an almshouse for twelve men and two women in 1600 and remained in use until 1930. Lyddington is 6 miles north of Corby, 1 mile east of the A6003.

Boothby Pagnell; Stamford All Saints). Carlton le Moorland had a secular founder with a personal interest as his daughter was a leper. These hospitals had an intercessory role in that they provided chantries to offer prayer for the souls of founders, benefactors and their families.

Newstead-by-Stamford had a change of use in that it began life allegedly in the late twelfth century as a hospital for the poor and sick, becoming a small priory for six canons in the mid-thirteenth century. The establishment of the hospital is verified by a charter of William de Albiny and his wife Agatha Trussebut c. 1225. At this date provision was for the maintenance of seven poor people. M J Franklin[2] thinks that it was 'common enough' for a layman to apply for an episcopal license to regularise his personal charity. The foundation document of Newstead[3], made in 1225/6, is valuable as it gives details of the provisions of, not only the Master and Infirmarer, but of the seven brothers who were the object of the charity. The food, rich in protein, seems exceedingly generous by any standards:-

'...each of the seven brothers shall receive every day one loaf made with salted flour or sieved flour and sprinkled with spice weighing fifty shillings and for them all to drink freely daily five gallons of ale. Besides this concerning the seven brothers, each pair daily shall receive for lunch a respectable dish of meat and drink and for dinner a 'relish' according to what the resources of the house can afford. In Lent each day each pair of brothers shall receive five herrings or six eggs together with his drink allowance, if not, four herrings at lunch time and for dinner according to propriety in a regular house. Should any of the seven be so sick that the aforesaid food is not good for him the Infirmarer, with the Master's knowledge, shall obtain what is fitting for him.'

The meaning of 'charity' can have various interpretations and is sometimes interpreted nowadays as 'love' but it must be remembered that in medieval days it was a duty. The seven corporal works of mercy are listed in Matthew 25:32-36 when Christ exhorts the disciples to look after others in order to gain salvation *i.e.* eternal life in the presence of God. *For when I was hungry you gave me food; when thirsty, you gave me drink; when I was a stranger you took me into your home, when naked you clothed me.....* According to the Roman Catholic Church of the day the alternative to salvation was damnation in hell and this was horrifying to the medieval mind. Purgatory was an intermediate Catholic staging post between heaven and hell and, during this phase in the soul's passage, prayers from earth could assist the promotion upwards.

People of the day were well-informed about the contemporary teaching on purgatory, not only from sermons but from written works such as *More's Supplication of Souls* and, for the illiterate, many verbal accounts of visions. Often the poor were considered to have suffered sufficiently on earth so, if they were virtuous, they might be exempt from purgatory. The rich, however, because they had been favoured on earth, must somehow survive purgatory if they were to reach heaven. The parable of Dives and Lazarus (Luke 16: 19-31) was frequently used to illustrate this belief. If Christ's injunction to give shelter and clothing and food were obeyed by those who had money it would assist them in gaining God's favour.

Therefore, it was thought, the founding of hospitals, or contributions towards them gave positive benefit to the donor. Another spiritual benefit could be gained by soliciting prayers for the soul of the donor by the establishment, with suitable endowment, of a chantry chapel. These were often attached to hospitals.

Yet another benefit could be by the receipt of an indulgence as a reward from the Catholic Church in return for a charitable foundation. Thus donors and occupants had something to gain. The occupants could pray for their benefactors but their own souls were not neglected. Thus acts of charity were medicine to the soul. Daily life in hospitals, therefore, included prayer by and for both inhabitants and donors. Prayer was a contribution to the divine life of the community. All the early hospitals would have a chapel incorporated into the building.

Indeed, before the Reformation, the emphasis was on spiritual rather than on physical health. It was believed that cleansing of the soul by confession, penitence and prayers made it more acceptable to God. It was, therefore, often stipulated that inhabitants were to attend mass daily and (as in an agreement between the Prior of Norwich and the townspeople of Yarmouth dated 1386) they were to say the Lord's Prayer and Ave 'with devotion' for the souls of past patrons.

The parable of Dives and Lazarus as depicted on the 12th century Romanesque frieze on Lincoln Cathedral. In the upper part of this sculpture the beggar Lazarus is carried up into Heaven by two angels while, below, the rich man Dives and his friends are driven into the gaping mouth of Hell by a demon. (Photo courtesy of the Dean and Chapter of Lincoln)

Bodily needs were obvious too (but perhaps less important than spiritual ones). One factor which affected need between the eleventh and fourteenth centuries was leprosy which raged through western Europe at this time. The term *leprosy* probably covered a range of diseases such as scrofula, tuberculosis, erysipelas, elephantiasis and other diseases contracted 'as a baneful result of a life stained by sin'. It has been suggested that a cross immunity exists between leprosy and tuberculosis as they are both caused by bacteria of the same genus. The leprosy of the bible was not the same disease as medieval leprosy which can be identified by skeletal remains. Nevertheless a stigma attached to leprosy which was sometimes associated with sin or witchcraft. A Malandry, or leper hospital, called the hospital of the Holy Innocents, was founded, probably by Remigius first bishop of Lincoln and can be dated from the early twelfth century by Charters of Henry I. The hospital, typically for such establishments, stood outside Lincoln near Cross o'Cliff Hill. At least seven hospitals were specifically for lepers in Lincolnshire in the period twelfth – fourteenth century. By the mid fifteenth century most leper hospitals were redundant.

The leprosy of the middle ages was sometimes sub-divided into four categories with variations on the following symptoms: hair fell off, the face became red and swollen and the voice hoarse; later the nostrils became deformed, the breath foul and the legs lost their feeling; nails enlarged and became scabby round the edges and pustules formed on the tongue; the skin was dry and covered in scabs. It was generally thought to be contagious yet St Hugh, Bishop of Lincoln 1186-1200, frequently consorted with lepers and washed their feet as an act of humility. Most leper hospitals contained a number of non-leprous inmates who must have had some immunity.

The Church cast out lepers, possibly as an act of preservation of the healthy members of the congregation. The priest exhorted the unfortunate outcasts to bear their affliction with penitence. The leper was taken to the church where part of the office for the dead was chanted and he was then conducted to the leper house or to his hut on the waste. Chancery actually devised a writ *de leproso amovendo* which made it necessary by law to remove the leper from society. He was thenceforth on the same footing as a criminal outlaw and debarred from inheritance.

A dedication to Saint Leonard was popular for leper hospitals as Leonard was said to be a healer and was revered as such. Two excavations have taken place in Grantham in the Spittlegate area (1857 and 1991) which suggest that a leper hospital known as St Leonard's may well have stood here. The evidence is not conclusive but is fairly substantial as a Christian burial site was found there with over forty skeletons orientated east-west. There was no recorded church there of the period but most of the pottery found on site dated from the thirteenth century which coincides with the known period of a leper house in Grantham. Three of the skeletons showed evidence of leprous changes to the bones[4] (see p 14).

It is hard to find a Lincolnshire account of daily life in a medieval hospital but it may be supposed to follow examples elsewhere in England and on the continent. Not all inhabitants were sick but generally they were aged or homeless. Prayer was of the first importance but beds and linen and nursing would also be provided. It would be normal to expect patients to share a bed but occasionally single beds might be specified. By the early sixteenth century hygiene regulations on the Italian model were incorporated into some foundation documents. Washing sheets, and sometimes patients, were part of the duties of the nurses who were often nuns with a spiritual duty to discharge as well as merely physical caring.

In June 1991 a medieval cemetery was discovered during the construction of a petrol station in the Spittlegate area of Grantham. The remains of 49 individuals were recovered, several of which were found to display the characteristic bone deformities of leprosy. The cemetery is presumed to be associated with St Margaret/Leonard's Hospital (gazetteer No. 13) recorded in Grantham in 1327.

Houses of pity (*Maisons Dieu* or *Domus Dei*) were small foundations resulting from endowments by lay persons. None of these houses can be identified for certain in Lincolnshire but 'Goddeshous' in Stamford might have been a *Domus Dei* and it was later referred to as such. Such places were, from evidence in other counties, often situated in houses or churchyards – the latter situation continued to be popular up to the twentieth century as a place in which to build almshouses.

Although the county is not rich in archaeological remains of medieval hospitals, some have left traces in street names such as Hospital Lane in Boston; St Leonard's Lane in Lincoln and St Giles' estate in Lincoln. St Giles (d. 710) was the patron saint of lepers, cripples and nursing mothers. He gave away his possessions to be shared among the poor so his name was particularly popular as a dedication. The occurrence of place-names or street names incorporating the elements Spital or Spittle is usually indicative of the site of a medieval hospital.

Browne's Hospital in Stamford is an excellent example of a late medieval foundation. It was built to provide succour for ten poor men and two women (the apostolic twelve) in 1475-6. Typically four ranges were built around a courtyard. The

St Giles - the patron saint of lepers cripples and nursing mothers. His name was a particularly popular dedication for medieval hospitals. This statue of the Saint in the Morning Chapel of Lincoln Cathedral was found on the site of St Giles Hospital, Lincoln, and shows him to be lame – his left leg is markedly shorter than his right. (Photo: D Peall)

main hospital building, of local stone with a fine tower, containing cubicled dormitories with a chapel at the eastern end was at the south side and this range survives. Patients could thus hear mass from their sick beds if necessary. This arrangement is generally known as an infirmary hall. The chapel rises the full height of the building. It has two tall three-light windows with castellated transoms. There are stalls with angels on the arm-rests and misericords which include angels, birds and mermaids. There is a cylindrical medieval almsbox. Some of the original stained glass survives in the entrance passage, including the arms of William Browne which consists of a stork rising from a bale of wool. It is thought that the glass may have been designed by John Glasier of Stamford who was the glass artist for windows at Tattershall church.

On the upper floor is the audit room, anteroom and confraters' room. These rooms were once used as Council Chambers. On the eastern side of the courtyard was a dining room, common room and priests' study. These are now demolished. The northern side, also demolished and replaced, held the kitchens, pantry and nurse's quarters. In the gardens were such buildings as the brewhouse, the washhouse, the knifehouse and coalhouses.

The main entrance at the west end was rebuilt in 1813 and much modified. In 1870 the architect James Fowler was employed to modernise the premises. The jettied upper floor above the west cloister was removed, a turret inserted and the west cloister extended. Pevsner describes the new cloister as 'nicely picturesque'. Fowler altered the porch and inserted a partition wall in the dormitory at the west end. He also designed the cottages in the courtyard which are the present almshouses.

It would be quite wrong to suggest that hospitals or bedehouses solved more than a tiny fraction of the problem of poverty. The earliest surviving minutes of Lincoln Council (1517) record the on-going problem of the poor. By 1531 a statute compelled 'impotent beggars' to have licences. Vagabonds were whipped and put in the stocks. The impotent poor were given alms by parish officials and a few charitable people left bequests to house deserving poor. The church, in the form of religious houses, was an instrument in the administration of charity.

This last provision was threatened by Henry VIII's sequestration of monastic property in the 1530s which included some hospitals. A way of allowing their continuance was a revival of the custom of 'feoffment to use' whereby land held by Church or Guild could be transferred to a sympathetic person and leased back to a proprietor or charitable body which could be a town council.

Before 1545 rich men who wished to ease their passage through purgatory left money for perpetual chantries, or the endowment of obits, but the less well-endowed could have their names inserted in the Sunday bede-roll on bequest of a more modest sum.

In 1545 the Chantries' Act abolished the concept of purgatory and chantry chapels became redundant at a stroke. Praying for the soul of the founder was one of the objects of hospitals, as in Browne's Hospital and others, so when this objective of foundation was removed would it threaten the hospitals? Fortunately Christian charity continued and God, or the officials of the

Browne's Hospital, Broad Street, Stamford

Browne's Hospital is said by Pevsner to be one of the best medieval hospitals in England. It was built in 1475/6 to provide accommodation for ten poor men and two women. William Browne died in 1489, but his Hospital survived the Reformation and continues as an almshouse to this day. The building originally comprised four ranges around a courtyard, the southern range (shown here) fronting onto Broad Street. This range housed the chapel (tall windows to the right) which occupies the full height of the building, with the cubicled dormitory in the hall below and service rooms above. Browne's Hospital was extensively restored by James Fowler in 1870. The porch and turret to the left belong to this period. (Photo: D Peall)

The former dormitory hall as it appears today – looking east towards the chapel Fowler removed the dormitory cubicles in 1870 to create this delightful open hall. The floor above, (which is an unusual feature for a medieval hospital) housed the audit room, anteroom and Confraters' room. (Photo: D Peall)

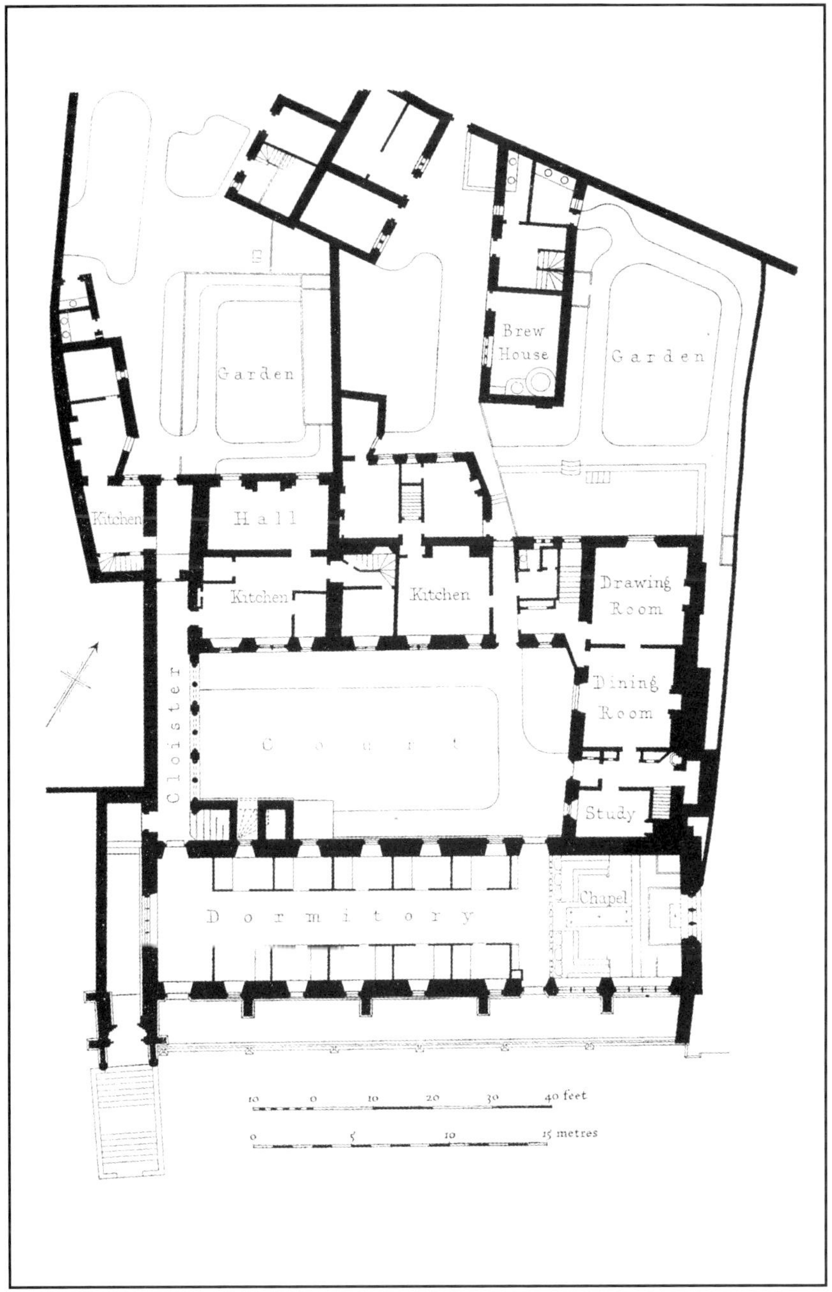

Prior to its 'restoration' by Fowler in 1870, Browne's Hospital typified the layout of a medieval hospital with four ranges of buildings around a courtyard. The plan of the building in 1858, prior to the alterations, is shown here (left). The south range housed the dormitory (with rooms above) and chapel with the cloister to its north. Service rooms formed the other ranges around an open courtyard. Fowler's alterations removed the north and east ranges completely (to give space for new accommodation) but retained and restored the dormitory, chapel and cloister.
© Crown copyright NMR after FT Dollman 1858

The chapel of Browne's Hospital retains some wonderful medieval fittings such as these seats (right) with their superbly carved hand rests (dragon like beast at inset, right) and misericords (mermaid, below).
(Photo: D Peall)

established church, still held sway and dictated where gratitude and duty lay. The Protestant era continued in the tradition of prayer and spirituality. At Lyddington, post-Reformation, prayers were part of the bedehouse regime. In the common hall at Lyddington occupants had to assemble three times daily for prayers. At the same place they were liable to fines for some sins such as sleeping with one's wife or blasphemy. This rule acknowledges that some occupants may be married but living apart from their spouses. Later, Truesdale's Hospital, Stamford, founded 1700, had rules relating to visits by wives, so the practice of married men being resident alone was not unknown.

Some poor did not want, or were not offered, recourse to protection by charity. The bands of beggars roaming the county were obviously a sore trial to good citizens. In the Lincoln of 1547 aldermen were to see that all valiant vagabonds, strong beggars and idle suspicious persons were punished and expelled from the city – but what of the impotent poor, the aged and infirm and widows? This constant problem had to be addressed by charity either administered by the parish or by individuals. In 1548 the poor were paraded in St Hugh's Croft in Lincoln and the able-bodied put to work; prisons and stocks were repaired in readiness for beggars and vagrants[5]. A statute of 1551/2 ordered mayors to appoint collectors of alms in each parish. The poor who had recourse to hospitals and almshouses were the fortunate ones indeed – the upper pauper class.

Browne's Hospital, Stamford, continued through the changes of the Reformation in a prayerful way. The Confrater was now a Church of England priest instead of Roman Catholic but the pattern of prayer and shelter continued. An insight into the procedure and politics of appointments at Browne's Hospital is found in documents in Lincolnshire Archives[6]. An affidavit of William Stukeley (a well-known antiquarian) who was Clerk (vicar) of the Church of All Saints in Stamford stated that he believed that Jacob Dodd, Clerk, died about the 11th day of November 1737. At the time of his death Dodd was Confrater of Browne's Hospital. Stukeley had the right and power, together with the Dean of Stamford, of nominating another Confrater within fourteen days of the death of the previous incumbent. This must have been a much sought-after post as the following account describes violent competition. Stukeley failed to nominate a candidate in the required time so the right fell on Francis Browne of Greatford, a descendant of the Founder. Browne nominated William Ross, Clerk, to the office of Confrater for the term of his natural life according to the Statutes, Ordinances and Constitutions of the Hospital. The appointment was solemnly confirmed in the chapel with Francis Browne, John Cawdron (Clerk and Warden), William Ross and the poor of the hospital present. Ross took the Oath of Admission and he was put into the 'real and actual possession of the said Confratership'. However, another contestant for the post was nominated – Henry Ridlington, Clerk, whose champions were William Spinks, said to be a descendant of William Browne and Thomas Lourd, a solicitor. Spinks came to the Hospital with his nominee, the lawyer and others and demanded the keys to the chapel. The Warden was out of town and had the keys with him so Spinks administered an oath to his candidate outside the chapel. On the next day, 8th December 1737, the false Confrater, with the Dean and many others, came to the hospital and, 'in very high and angry words demanded of the warden the keys of the chapel and the poor to attend there' in order to admit the new Confrater. The affidavit refers to the 'pretended nomination' of 'the pretended heir'. The Dean was requested to desist from 'such violent and tumultuous proceedings'. There followed an attempt to break the chapel door down but the lock withstood. Again an oath was administered to the pretended nominee outside the chapel. A person of the invading party then spied a ladder near the chapel and the nominee climbed up and entered the chapel 'through the bars'. Another oath was administered by the Dean outside the chapel with the nominee responding from inside.

Ten days later the Dean appeared at the hospital again with a Mr Hurd and Thomas Alcock, Mayor of Stamford, and others 'in a very outrageous and tumultuous manner demanding the keys of the chapel and the poor'. This was refused and the undignified gentlemen again threatened to break down the chapel door. Constables who lodged at a neighbouring house were called. Mr Spinks the 'pretended heir to the Founder' was advised to take his remedy at Law and to desist from violence.

Another oath was administered two days later on the stairs leading to the Great Room (Audit Room) in the presence of the Dean, the Mayor and the Town Clerk; the keys were again refused. So keen was Ridlington to obtain the post that he later petitioned Lord Hardwick the Lord High Chancellor to support his case. He was unsuccessful and the Revd W Ross held the confratership from 1738-1744.

In summary, the earliest forms of charity housing were known as Hospitals. They were either attached to a monastery or were church foundations such as Partney (founded c. 1115) and Elsham (founded prior to 1166). These establishments were for the benefit of the poor and the sick. The first known Leper Hospital in the county (*La Malanderie* in Lincoln) appeared in the early twelfth century and foundations for the aid of lepers continued for a couple of centuries. As the concept of purgatory developed into an episcopal industry hospitals were founded for the prime object of praying for the soul of a founder through chantries. Boothby Pagnell is an early example of this, founded by John Paynell at the end of the twelfth century. Ralph Cromwell's foundation in 1440 is another early foundation by an individual in the county although there could have been an earlier one in Tattershall founded by Maud Cromwell, grandmother of Ralph. Browne's Hospital, Stamford was founded in 1483 – fifty years before the Reformation and continued through the Protestant changes to the present day. The hospitals up to the mid-sixteenth century had the twin motives of cure for body and soul. By the time of the Reformation and the abolition of chantries hospitals were becoming known as Bedehouses – a name which is synonymous with Almshouses.

In all the gazetteers that follow, the status of the building is indicated by a letter, thus:

X *Building no longer exists*

S *Still in use as an almshouse (but may be a rebuilding of original)*

P *Building survives but not now in use as an almshouse*

GAZETTEER

Hospitals founded 1100 - 1550

A = Leper house B = Almshouse
C = Wayfarers and pilgrims D = Sick other than lepers
E = Other including not known.

1. **Barton on Humber: St Leonard's Hospital** was founded in 1259. No more is known. (E) (X)

2. **Boothby Pagnell: Hospital of St John the Baptist** was founded towards the end of the twelfth century either by John Paynell or Hugh of Boothby. It was intended for poor leprous women. The chapel must have served as a chantry as there was a chantry certificate. It ceased as a hospital and the chapel was used as a parochial chapel for the hamlet early in the fourteenth century. (A) (X)

3. **Boston: St John the Baptist** was founded before 1282 'without' the town. At that time it had revenue to maintain 'several' poor men. It was said to be still in existence in 1480. (B) (X)

4. **Brigg: St John the Baptist** founded 1422 was an almshouse for men. There was originally a priest warden, a chaplain and seven poor men. It was dissolved at the Reformation. (B) (X) (see also, entries for Glanford Brigg and Glandford Bridge)

5. **Carlton le Moorland: Hospital of St Lazarus** founded before 1301. The Order of St Lazarus worked for lepers during the second crusade. The founder of this hospital, Elias de Amundeville, was interested in the welfare of lepers as his daughter was a leper. (A) (X)

6. **Eagle:** founded before 1154 for sick or aged members of the order of Templars[7]. (E) (X)

7. **Edenham:** Hospital was founded before 1319. Nothing else is known. (E) (X)

8. **Elsham: SS Mary and Edmund** was founded before 1166 for the poor, aged sick and survived into the thirteenth century; it was dependent on the Austins. It was said to be founded by Lady Beatrice D'Munderville who invited seven Austin canons from France to care for the sick. It was the beginning of Elsham Priory, an Augustinian house. (D) (X)

9. **Gainsborough:** founded in 1495, apparently as an almshouse; nothing else known. (B) (X)

10. **Gedney: St Thomas Martyr's Almshouses** – foundation date unknown but it was known to exist in 1339 but had ceased to exist by 1341. It supported five paupers and was served by a canon of North Creake Abbey. (B) (X)

11. **Glanford Brigg:** or **Wrawby Hospital** was founded by Adam Paynell towards the end of the twelfth century and placed in charge of the Abbot of Selby, Yorkshire. It was to be an almshouse for the poor but its dedication is unknown. In 1236 it had ceased to be used as an almshouse and the abbot was using it for his own purposes. An attempt was made to restore its use by Papal

bull of Gregory IX but it is not known how long, if at all, the reform lasted. (B) (X)

12. Glandford Bridge: a hospital was founded here in 1422 by Sir William Tyrwhitt. It was dedicated to **St John the Baptist** to provide maintenance for seven poor men and two chaplains (one to be master). They were to pray continually for the souls of King Henry VI and the founder. (B) (X)

13. Grantham: Hospital of St Margaret founded before 1328. This appears to be the same hospital as St Leonard's so the latter could be a rededication. The Hospital of St Margaret by Grantham is mentioned in the Patent Rolls for 1327-1330 but not after that. Excavations of a Christian burial site that could belong to the hospital were carried out in 1857 and 1991. Three of the skeletons found in the more recent excavation showed positive evidence of leprosy. The Hundred Rolls for 1272/3 make mention of an unfortunate inmate who was hanged for stealing a sheepskin. *'Richard le Syneker of the hospital ouside Grantham came like a thief by night to the house of Thomas of Swaneton, in Grantham, and broke the gate of his tannery.'* The aggrieved tanner raised hue and cry and pursued Richard to the hospital where he arrested him and handed him over to the King's bailiff. Two days later he was hanged. The land and chapel were acquired by the Crown at the Dissolution. (A) (X)

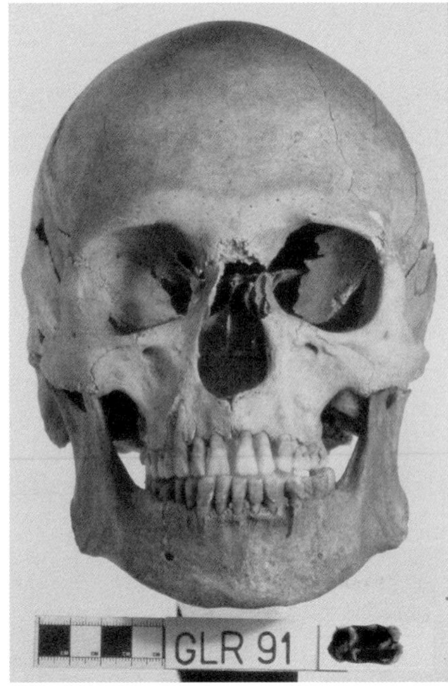

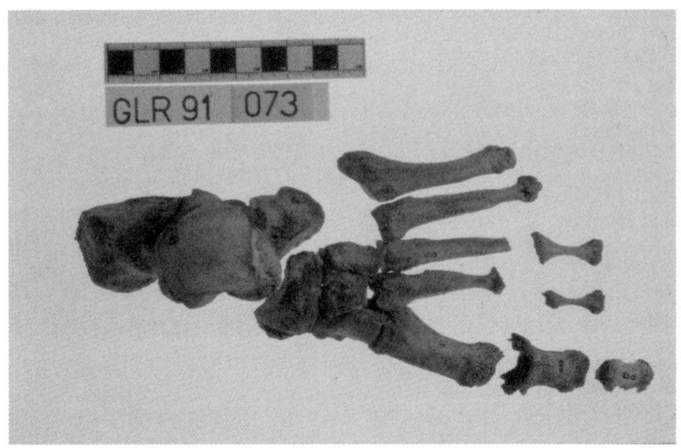

Some of the bones from the Spittlegate Cemetery (see St Margaret's, No. 13) in Grantham (excavated in 1991) showed characteristic signs of leprosy. The skull has a modified nasal aperture and the foot bones (of skeleton 073) show leprous changes with 'pencilling' of the metatarsals and 'waisting' of the phalanges. (Photo: The Dept. of Archaeology & Prehistory, Sheffield University)

14. Grimsby: Hospital of Saint Mary Magdalen and St Leger was founded in the thirteenth century. It was intended for male or female lepers. In 1291 Bishop Sutton issued an indulgence to people who would give 'to the supreme need of the miserable poor lepers'. The last mention is in 1336 when the king granted protection to those collecting alms for the hospital. It possibly became extinct at the time of the Black Death. (A) (X)

15. Grimsby: St John's Hospital founded before 1389. (E) (X)

16. Holbeach: Hospital of All Saints founded by Sir John of Kirton in 1351 to sustain the warden and fifteen poor people. It had ceased to exist by the Reformation. (B) (X)

17. Langworth: St Margaret's Hospital for Lepers. Little is known. It existed in 1313. (A) (X)

18. Lincoln: Holy Innocents without the city is the earliest hospital in the county dating from the early twelfth century. It was situated on the western edge of South Common a few hundred yards beyond the old southern entrance to the suburb of Wigford. Charters of Henry I called it *La Malanderie*.

The hospital stood on a site of about fifteen acres. There were certainly orchards and gardens and we know that 'there were timber trees thereon'. The hospital appears to have been composed of a range of one-storied buildings (inmates' cells) grouped in a rough rectangle. Utility buildings, such as

In 1862 the railway line from Lincoln to Honiton cut through the site of Holy Innocents' Hospital on Lincoln's South Common. A coffin lid or tombstone dedicated to Yvette de Rauceby, wife of William de Rauceby, was unearthed during the work and is now in St Denys Church, Sleaford. The inscription, which begins top right, is in Old French and may be translated as: "You who here pass by, pray for the soul of Yvette, the honoured wife of W de Rauceby. May God have mercy on her soul." (Drawn by David Hopkins)

a bakery, brewhouse and granary, would have been separate buildings nearby. The two-storied dining hall was called '*Le Kychenhalle*'. The parish church of Holy Innocents served both the parish and the lepers. There was also a chapel of St Mary Magdalene. The whole campus was known as the Malandry fields.

The early intentions and administration were doubtless good but things did deteriorate badly over the centuries and, by the time of the reformation, there appeared to have been a certain amount of corruption, mainly by the wardens.

In the mid-twelfth century each male leper received a cell and curtilage (marked surrounding area) and a sum of tenpence halfpenny a week (females had only ninepence) with an allowances of forty bundles of turfs for fuel. The two chaplains received accommodation, turfs and fifteen pence per week and the clerk, twelve pence per week. Extra income was obtained by the grisly requirement that inhabitants should bury the bodies of persons hanged on the city gallows at Canwick Hill.

In 1230 the first of several royal protections for the hospital appeared which gives an insight into how funds might be raised to aid the lepers apart from the original grants of land. It granted protection to the brethren, or their clerks who might preach on their behalf or seek alms for them. The protection was needed, apparently against royal officials who might hinder them. Matters had started to become difficult.

By 1274 things were looking bad and the hospital was in danger of dissolution. The warden was removed as 'he had wasted the goods of the foundation'. One poor woman whose husband was a leper fell foul of bailiffs when she was only trying to help her husband who lived in the hospital. He was near to death and fainted on the 'spitalgrene' so his wife had him carried to her house where he was seen by a priest before he died. The bailiffs then imprisoned the wife on a charge of suffocating her husband and she was only released on payment of seven shillings and fourpence and three hens.

Another woman, an inmate called Margaret de Burgh had an extraordinary experience. Her son was a thief and she hid him in her cell when he was fleeing with stolen property. The concealment was discovered and she was charged with harbouring him and subsequently hanged. Here the tale enters into the world of the quixotic but the facts are recorded in the Civil Pleas Rolls. Margaret's body was taken to the Malandry to be buried but she recovered and lived for some years with the benefit of a royal pardon.

There were connections with royalty from the start of this foundation. Edward I, who often visited Lincoln and indeed held a parliament here in the cathedral chapter house, granted Margaret's pardon and seems to have taken an interest in the hospital. It would appear that, through the thirteenth, fourteenth and fifteenth century the hospital was unfortunate in its wardens, many of whom sought to better themselves. Edward I clarified the duties of the chaplains and instructed royal officers to assist the brethren in collecting alms. Bishop Sutton, on these instructions, specified that hospital collectors should be allowed to collect in churches and, on three Sundays a year, be allowed to speak to the congregations.

We know that, by 1307, not all the inmates were lepers as one John, son of Peter, who was a aged arms contractor was granted the livery of the brethren and life protection of the hospital as a reward for service in Scotland and Wales. He had lost his horses and carts in the Welsh rebellion, was 80 years old and blind and obviously in need of help.

The wardenship was regarded as a desirable sinecure which could even be held in plurality with other lucrative offices. The pay of a shilling a week was better than a pay of a skilled craftsman. In addition timber could be sold and the almsbox raided. Visitation records give details of such temptations.

By 1301 the hospital was described as being 'much decayed for want of good governance' and two years later an inquest was conducted. The hospital staggered on with its administrative troubles and it appears that Edward II also took an interest in it when he visited the city in 1315-16. An ecclesiastical visitation and verdict by a local jury found many faults. In 1323 after many changes of wardenship there were accusations that people representing themselves falsely as authorised to collect alms for the hospital were, in fact, fraudsters. By 1336 the wardenship was openly a perquisite of royal clerks.

The hospital, however, was still accepting inmates – now rather in the nature of boarders (non-lepers) such as one Alice Hotot for whom a residence was built. Pensions or corrodies could be bought with a lump sum and Alice gained the right to 10½d per week plus forty loads of turf annually, straw for her bed and maintenance of her dwelling by the warden and brethren.

In the 1330s troubles continued; there were nine brethren and sisters of whom only one was a leper and he had bought his place there for 100 shillings (contrary to the terms of the foundation). The seven women had also paid for admittance. Episcopal visitations continued to make bad reports.

In the 1340s corruption appeared to be rife and there are reports of vestments and a chalice stolen by wardens and their staff. 1349 was the year of the Black Death and many inhabitants of Lincoln succumbed but we do not know the death rate of the inmates of the hospital. However we do know that the then-Warden, John de Nessefield survived.

A royal charter of Henry VI attached the hospital to the Leper House at Burton Lazars in Leicestershire. So the leper house limped on, sometimes in a state of corruption, sharing a reputation for scandal that overtook many religious institutions long before the Reformation. By 1534 when the order of St Lazarus (of which the hospital was a part) was suppressed, the revenue for that year was £30. 13s. 4d. *C.* 1549 the land was granted to John Dudley, Lord Lisle. A hoard of 780 silver coins (The Malandry Coin Hoard) of Henry I's reign was found on the site in 1972 and was sent to the British Museum. Could the hoard be evidence of the 'jobbery and peculation' recorded in the history of this hospital?[8] (A) (X)

19. Lincoln: St Sepulchre; founded 1094-1123, for poor, aged sick. It was in the area to the south of Altham Terrace. After 1148 it became a Gilbertine Priory dedicated to St Sepulchre and SS James and Catherine for the care of the sick. It was discontinued at the Reformation. (D) (X)

20. Lincoln: St Giles' Hospital: probably founded some time in the thirteenth century by an unknown founder. It was situated on Wragby Road at the east end of the present Lindum Cricket ground. By 1280 Oliver Sutton, Dean of Lincoln, assigned the house with its revenues to the support of the vicars choral. It was intended for the poor and in the fourteenth century endowments were added in order that past servants of the cathedral might have preference over other applicants. They were to receive ½d daily for food and 4 shillings yearly for clothing. The hospital was provided with an indenture dated 1564 between Sir William Tailboys (Canon of the cathedral) and the vicars choral. Five poor men residing in the house should receive 4d weekly and 4/8d at Christmas to buy a gown or livery cloak. The overplus, if any, to be applied to the repair of the house. It fell into ruins in the eighteenth century but was still marked on nineteenth century maps as a hospital. The final fragments were demolished in 1927 and some ashlar dressings were incorporated into St Giles' Church, Lamb Gardens in 1933-36. A statue of St Giles with a lame foot was excavated on the site and now stands in the Morning Chapel of Lincoln Cathedral. (B) (X)

21. Lincoln: The Hospital of St Leonard Without the Castle, was founded some time before 1300 for lepers and other sick persons. It is thought to have been in the area of The Lawn. In 1300 Bishop Dalderby called on rectors and vicars of Lincoln and Stowe deaneries to make collections in aid of it. An indulgence for its support was made in 1311 since when nothing further is known of it. (A) (X)

22. Lincoln: St Mary Magdalene Almshouse for the poor was in existence before 1311 when Edward II sent one of his old servants to receive 'the necessaries of life' there. It was still standing in 1402 since when nothing is known. It was also called St Mary Blessed Virgin and St Mary Magdalen according to Knowles and Hadcock. (B) (X)

23. Lincoln: Hospital of St Bartholomew Without the Castle – known to exist between 1314-1331 for lepers and other sick people. The church and Hospital of St Bartholomew was situated on the site of The Lawn and there seems to be some confusion between this and the Hospital of St Leonard without the castle. Mass burials of the 13th century were found on the site in 1984/85.[9] Records refer to licences to collect alms granted by the bishop or the king. A hospital chapel was built by the Dean and Chapter between 1466 and 1470 with the stone from the fallen steeple of St Bartholomew's church. The hospital chapel is probably shown on Buck's 1743 'South-west prospect' drawing but it was certainly demolished by 1777. (A & D) (X)

24. Louth: foundation and dedication are not known but a hospital was in existence in 1314. It was for lepers – possibly ceased to exist at the time of the Black Death. (A) (X)

25. Louth: Trinity Bedehouse founded in the sixteenth century as an almshouse – date of dissolution not known. (B) (X)

26. Louth: Hospital of St Mary Blessed Virgin founded in the sixteenth century; nothing else is known. (F) (X)

27. Mere: (parish of Dunston) Hospital of St John the Baptist was founded *c.* 1244 by Simon de Roppele. This hospital was one of the few which survived the Reformation although it later had a scandalous history. It was for lepers and almshouse men. There is a map in the Ross Collection at Lincolnshire Archives Office which attempts to show the location.

A memorandum of a lease of 1553 mentions 'all the manor and hospital of Mere etc. with the Mere Wood or Mere Okes containing 5 acres'. At this date the number of bedesmen was reduced from 13 to three persons and the warden. In 1665 the Hospital still existed for 'some' poor men. 'The revenues are considerable but said to be perverted.'[10] The income from the land continued and by 1680 six poor men were paid £4 per annum. The Charity Commissioners of 1837 commented that the poor appear to have become recipients of dole rather than shelter but the nominal warden had not only the annual £8 salary but 'extremely profitable' leases which 'to the present day have gone exclusively into the pocket of the warden'. It appears that by 1786 the Hospital had long fallen into decay but the income continued to accrue. At that date the Bishop of Ely was warden and collected his salary and rental money although he had no duties. The Commission referred to 'obstacles thrown in this Inquiry by the Cathedral dignitaries'.

The nineteenth century 'wardens' were the Revd John Pretyman (grandson of a bishop of Lincoln) and his relative Revd Richard Pretyman. A fund of £5000 had accumulated by the mid nineteenth century as the Hospital estate still held land worth £1350 per annum. The case was referred to the Court of Chancery and the surviving Pretyman had to pay a £1000 fine. Both he and the lessee of the land were told that: 'neither of them should in future have anything to do with the revenues of the hospital'. (A & B) (X)

28. Newstead-by-Stamford: Hospital of St Mary was founded before 1200 for seven poor and infirm persons (later thirteen). It became an Augustinian priory. The first recorded Master of the hospital was Walter. C. 1225, (when Master Adam was Master) the founder, William of Albiny and his wife Agatha Trussebut, had a charter drawn up with the consent of Bishop Hugh of Lincoln and Archdeacon Robert which listed the endowment in the form of arable, pasture and personal tithes. (B) (X)

29. Partney: Hospital of St Mary Magdalene was built soon after 1115; it was dependent on the Benedictine Bardney Abbey. It is uncertain whether it was intended for sick or for aged poor. By the fourteenth century it had ceased to be a hospital and became a small cell of the abbey. Stocker[11] feels that the foundation could have been based around an older centre or pre-existing community. (D) (X)

30. Sempringham is listed by Knowles and Hadcock with an undated reference to a leper hospital but this may refer to the Gilbertine priory at Clattercote (Oxon.) which had a leper hospital attached. (E) (X)

31. Skirbeck Hospital near Boston: was dedicated to St Leonard some time before 1230 when it was granted to the Knights Hospitallers of St John of Jerusalem who held it until the suppression of religious houses. During this time it was known as St John's Hospital. It was for the use of twenty poor people and was endowed with lands sufficient to maintain three priests at Skirbeck and one at Fleet. In addition to the twenty residents, forty more were relieved at the gate every day. It had become a preceptory by 1400. It was suppressed by Henry VIII and all possessions were granted to the Duke of Suffolk in 1541. Shortly after this it was passed to the new Corporation of Boston. The nearby footbridge over the Maud Foster Drain is still called Hospital Bridge. (A) (X)

32. Sleaford: former almshouses are recorded in Westgate – there is now no trace. In a survey of Lord Hussey's possessions in 1538[12] are listed: *'bedehouses or almshouses ... there is 2 cottages called bede houses in the holding of Agnes paben(er) & John Appilby & is woryh by yere 8s.'* (B) (X)

33. Spalding: A hospital for lepers dedicated to **St Nicholas** – founder and date of foundation unknown; it may have had a connection with a priory of the same dedication. The hospital was in existence in 1323 – after which nothing is known. It could have become extinct at the time of the Black Death. (A) (X)

34. Spital in the Street (parish of Glentworth): hospital built in 1396 by **Thomas Aston** canon of Lincoln. This house was not suppressed among the hospitals generally at the Reformation. In 1837 the Charity Commissioners had some difficulty getting evidence from R Swan, the agent of the nominal warden of the Hospital, the Revd J Pretyman. The dean and chapter claimed immunity from giving evidence. The Charity Commissioners stated, to the best of their knowledge, that the earliest reference to the hospital was in a patent of Edward II, 1323, but, at that date, they concluded the premises were probably for the entertainment of pilgrims and wayfaring people. In fact, as the hospital was a possession of the Knights Templar it would have been suppressed in 1312 along with all property of the order throughout Europe. In 1396 Thomas de Aston made additions to the hospital, 'rebuilt for the lodgement of the poor men'. The wording in the patent document, *in augmentation of the maintenance of the poor there dwelling,* suggests that some provision for the poor had been made by a former founder. In 1396 rules[13] relating to the hospital state that 'Every poor man of the seven to receive 7d per week, and if any chaplain reduced by age to poverty wished to spend his days there for reverence to his state and order he should receive 10d per week and be accounted one of the seven.' In 1598 it was described as 'an ancient hospital for relief of the poor'. In 1615 Sir William Wray was maintaining the hospital but his grandson, Sir John Wray, denied the rents and burnt the decree. The hospital continued poorly. In the Parliamentary Returns for 1786 it is stated that, in the parish of Hemswell, there is a hospital for four poor widows who receive 8/- per month. By 1837 two tenements remained but they were not occupied by pensioners. The building, on the west side of the chapel, had recently been repaired by the landlord of the Spital Inn as no-one appeared to claim it and he had placed his ostler in one and another servant in the second cottage. The building still remained in the ownership of the Spital

The chapel and almshouse at Spital in the Street – drawn around 1803.
The inscription on the almshouse reads DEO et DIVITIBUS A.D. 1620.

Charity, who, after the closure of the inn in about 1860, used it to accommodate a variety of tenants – often the sexton who was responsible for the maintenance of the chapel. In 1868 the advowson of Skellingthorpe previously vested in the patronage of the Master of Spital Hospital was sold for £1350 and assigned to the trustees of the Spital Charities. Pevsner states, 'the humble cottages' on the site were built in 1620. The cottages are now privately owned as the Spital Charity sold off the almshouses (by then one building) in about 1960. The Spital Charity still pays out-pensions to people in the district. (B) (P)

35. Stamford: Hospital of St Leger was founded before 1199. Nothing else is known. Some writers, *e.g.* Hartley and Rogers[14], doubt if St Leger's existed in Stamford. (E) (X)

36. Stamford: St Sepulchre was a house of Austin canons established before 1189 and this was later converted into a hospital for poor pilgrims. It could have been connected with the Knights Hospitallers. Nothing is heard of it after 1227. (C) (X)

37. Stamford: Hospital of St John the Baptist and St Thomas the Martyr, founded *c.* 1170. A few fragments of Norman masonry are still visible on the east corner of the main range facing the river. This hospital was first under the patronage of The Guild of Palmers and was later controlled by the abbey of Peterborough. The building was described in 1299 as consisting of a hall, chamber, solar, kitchen and bakehouse with other chambers for the chaplain and the sick. The building possessed a burial yard. In 1595 the hospital was divided and part of it remained as a 'beadhouse'. Lord Burghley incorporated some of the structure into his almshouses *c.* 1597. (C & B) (X)

38. Stamford: St Giles' Hospital (also sometimes called **St Leonard's**) outside Stamford, founded at an unknown date but it was in existence before 1304 when a chaplain and lepers were in residence. It could have been on a site approximately 42 High Street in modern Stamford. It is often linked with the larger St Thomas and St John the Baptist Hospital. It was under royal protection in the thirteenth century. It may have continued as some sort of hospital through the fourteenth, fifteenth and sixteenth centuries. In 1676 a building on the site (presumably a replacement) was referred to as 'the Spittlehouse'. The Fryer's Hospital (founded 1833) continued poor relief in the area. (E) (X)

39. Not allocated

40. Stamford: Hospital of St Giles Outside the Town: it was for the use of lepers but little else is known. It existed at least between 1304 -1332 and there is a later reference in 1516-17. There seems to be some confusion with St Leonard's Hospital. Also Hartley and Rogers say that a reference to St George's Hospital clearly refers to St Giles Hospital. (A) (X)

41. Stamford: Hospital of All Saints, Broad Street (now known as **Browne's Hospital**). It was founded by William Browne, merchant of the staple of Calais, in 1485 for the support of two chaplains and the distribution of alms to twelve poor persons who should pray for the soul of the founder in the Catholic tradition. It was for ten poor men and two women. It was refounded in 1610. There are four ranges of buildings round a courtyard with dormitory and chapel; there is some 1870 work by James Fowler who built a new clock tower and rearranged the medieval stained glass in the chapel which contains a medieval oak screen and misericords. Wooden cubicles which formed the living quarter in the common room have been removed. This room is now the Board Room. Originally five cubicles were on either side of a wide aisle. Sick and dying residents could be placed in cubicles near to the chapel and still hear mass. A similar arrangement can still be seen in the hospital at Beaune, near Dijon in France. Kelly's 1905 Directory says it was founded by William Browne in 1483-5 and completed in 1493. The foundation was for a warden, confrater and twelve poor. There was a rich endowment of 1,935 acres. The residue of the income went to Stamford Endowed Schools. Modern residents live in eleven flats made within the 1870 stone cottages, designed by Fowler, built around the quadrangle. These were modernised in 1963. A prayer for the founders is still said each week in the chapel: *O Lord God, the Resurrection and the life of all that believe in Thee, Who art to be praised in the Dead as in the Living, we give Thee hearty thanks for our Founders, William Browne, Thomas Stokke, King James the First and all our other benefactors, by whose gifts we are here nourished to piety and goodness; beseeching Thee that we, rightly using these Thy benefits to Thy Glory, may together with all Thy faithful, be brought to Immortal Glory of Thy Resurrection through Jesus Christ our Lord.* This prayer, with its Protestant wording (Resurrection through Jesus Christ) must have been composed after the Reformation and Counter-Reformation. It contrasts with the Catholic words on the brass of William and Margaret Browne's tomb: *Dere lady help at nede.* Today both men and women are residents. A warden lives on the premises still but the confrater (Brother in Christ), who is generally a retired clergyman now lives outside. A service is still held in the chapel each week. The uniform was last worn *c.* 1950; it consisted of a dark blue cutaway jacket, waistcoat, brown corduroy breeches, black leather leggings and black boots. The hospital offers accommodation to people over 60 who live in or have relations in the Stamford area. (B) (S)

42. Stamford: *Domus Dei*: There is a reference in deeds from 1414-1500 as 'Goddeshous' in Eastgate (St Paul's Street). Nothing else is known. (C) (X)

43. Stamford: St Helen's Hospital. No evidence for this place exists during its life – only a mention in 1547 after its dissolution.[15] (E) (X)

44. Stamford: a Callis is known to have existed in 1466 in St Peter's (or All Saints) parish. Later it might have become Williamson's Hospital. (X)

45. Tattershall: Bedehouses, founded under Tattershall College *c.* 1440 by Ralph Cromwell for thirteen poor people and endowed with £30.6.8d. yearly. An almshouse is said to have existed here before, founded by Ralph Cromwell's grandmother Maud. His foundation was a rebuilding or rather the transfer of a timber-framed building from another site to Tattershall to be used as almshouses. Present buildings are early seventeenth century in brick and reused limestone masonry with pantile roof over a simple rafter. Brick is laid in English bond. There are four pairs of chimneys and a single chimney on each gable end. Archaeological recording carried out in 1995 during refurbishment of the almshouses enabled a conjectural plan of the seventeenth century structure to be proposed, each dwelling having a single room with doorway and a fireplace. In 1834 a further endowment of

The Tattershall Bedehouses: *The first almshouse at Tattershall (for 12 poor people) was founded before 1419 by Maud de Bernack, the grandmother of Ralph Lord Cromwell. Cromwell is best known for his startling refurbishment of Tattershall Castle, but he also commissioned the building of the collegiate church and a new almshouse. The Cromwell Bedehouse, built in c. 1440, was a timber framed hall 172 feet long by 19 feet wide having chambers for thirteen inmates, with a hall at the west end and a chapel at the east. The almshouses were rebuilt again in the seventeenth century, roughly to the shape of the building we see today. By the 1960s the bedehouses provided ten single roomed dwellings. A further refurbishment in 1966 combined pairs of rooms to form five two-roomed apartments. The Tattershall Bedehouses, in their traditional position beside the church, are still in use today.*

£7.10s per annum was added by Hirst Gibson to be given in calico and money. At one time the houses were known as 'Gallery Row'. In 1911 new rules were drawn up which included the following: *Carpets, Mats, etc., must not be hung over the Church railings and 'Slops' and other refuse must not be thrown over the Church or Field Fences. No occupant may give permission to strangers or others to use the Bede House Conveniences. Nor may occupants store bicycles for the public, or provide them with tea, or in any way whatsoever cater for them on Bede House premises.* In the 1960s much restoration and modernisation was done and the ten dwellings were converted into five. A new Lincolnshire pantile roof was installed and back access was made to each house. (B) (S)

46. Thornton Curtis: Hospital dedicated to **St James** - without the walls of the abbey. It is known that there was a hospital on the site when a college was founded there by Henry VIII. It included the care of the aged and those who had spent their lives in the service of the realm. This appears to include old soldiers. The college was suppressed by Edward VI. Nimon Gibon, trumpeter to Queen Elizabeth, petitioned on 1 August 1595 for the vacant almsroom in Thornton College; he had, 'served [in] the Low Countries under the Earl of Leicester'; the petition was granted. An old woman of the college called Mother Gelly was buried there in 1599/1600 and another called Pegge Foote buried out of the college in March 1601/2. That is the last reference to almshouse residents.[16] (B) (X)

47. Threekingham: Hospital of St Lazarus for lepers; founded before 1319. Nothing else known. (A) (X)

48. Walcot: Hospital of St Leonard for lepers. Little is known. It existed in 1311. (A) (X)

1550 - 1800 : The Evolution of the Almshouse

Protestant England continued with the tradition of almshouse foundations with religious, and sometimes educational ethos, for example, Louth King Edward's, 1551; Branston, 1553; Wrangle, 1555 and Lincoln St Giles, 1564.

Endowments for almshouses and schools were administered by appointed trustees with church, civic or familial connections. The trusteeship system continues to work to this day, now regulated by The Charity Commissioners but scandals could and did occur, such as at Spital Hospital and Mere Hospital at Branston. Anthony Trollope, who had Lincolnshire connections, wrote of a typical Victorian scandal which was thought to have been based on Winchester's Hospital of St Cross where the Revd Francis North, son of a bishop and nephew of the Prime Minister, Lord North, was appointed to the hospital's mastership. He pocketed most of the money from the foundation over the forty years during which he was master. The Charity Commission was set up soon after the scandal in 1855. Trollope's book[1], published that year, sets the scene of a typical hospital or almshouse:

In the year 1434 there died at Barchester one John Hiram, who had made money in the town as a woolstapler, and in his will he left the house in which he died and certain meadows and closes near the town, still called Hiram's Butts, and Hiram's Patch, for the support of twelve superannuated wool-carders, all of whom should have been born and bred and spent their days in Barchester; he also appointed that an almshouse should be built for their abode, with a fitting residence for a warden, which warden was also to receive a certain sum annually out of the rents of the said butts and patches........

From that day to this the charity had gone on and prospered - at least, the charity had gone on, and the estates had prospered. Wool-carding in Barchester there was no longer any; so the bishop, dean, and warden, who took it in turn to put in the old men, generally appointed some hangers-on of their own; worn-out gardeners, decrepit grave-diggers, or octogenarian sextons, who thankfully received a comfortable lodging and one shilling and fourpence a day, such being the stipend to which, under the will of John Hiram, they were declared to be entitled.

The dispute, which is the core of the story, arises when the bedesmen are goaded into discontent at the small sum they receive from the charity (for which they were formerly grateful) in comparison with the £800 per annum which the warden received. The will is re-examined; the warden, who is a naive clergyman with no dishonest intent, resigns and the bedesmen are no better off. The book gives a picture of the division between the educated gentlemen of the day dispensing charity in a way perhaps not now acceptable. The question of changing times and necessary adjustments to founders' ancient instructions is addressed.

I cannot help seeing, that the affairs of the hospital are not arranged according to the will of the founder.

None of such institutions are, Mr Harding, nor can they be; the altered circumstances in which we live do not admit of it.

The foundation of almshouses was patchy and at no time did it provide for all necessitous people. It could be said to be a nominal social-housing arrangement of the early modern era.

In Lincoln a statute of 1551/2 ordered mayors to appoint collectors of alms in each parish. In 1560 a beadle of the beggars was appointed as a parish officer to oversee the poor and idle in the city. The City of Lincoln, in common with other places besieged by beggars and vagabonds, was willing to maintain its own poor but jibbed at supporting the poor who came from other places.

In 1586/7 plague ravaged Lincoln and poverty was again an urgent issue. Freemen were ordered to expel tenants who had not lived in the city for three years. No more strange poor were to be taken as tenants and a blacksmith who had put up a mud building to shelter homeless beggars was ordered to pull it down.

A project for a House of Industry, first mooted in 1578, was revived in the 1580s and a room was provided in the lower floor of Greyfriars where the poor could spin and knit. This was known as the Jersey School. This 'school' survived until 1629 and examples of efforts to provide work for the poor to maintain themselves are found in most sizeable parishes. (The Jersey School was revived in 1661.)

In 1631 the Law of Settlement caused poor travellers to carry a certificate of settlement from their home parish and they could be returned there if they became a charge on another parish. The housing problems of the hordes of migrant

Greyfriars in Broadgate, Lincoln, is thought to have been the infirmary of Lincoln's thirteenth century Franciscan Friary. In the 1580s a room was provided on the ground floor of Greyfriars for a 'House of Industry' (known as the Jersey School) where the poor could spin and knit.

poor were resolved partly by this Act and partly by ignoring the problem but the sheer numbers of people requiring shelter caused action to be taken in towns.

Grantham had a set of rules later adopted by Lincoln in 1636. Francis Hill wrote[2]: 'The building of cottages, the conversion of barns, stables and outhouses, and the division of houses had facilitated a great confluence and resort of poor people from foreign places.' To remedy this anyone who wished to take in a stranger tenant must have the written consent of the mayor and council.

By the seventeenth century, the use of the term 'bedesman' or 'bedeswoman' does not necessarily imply that the recipient lived in bedehouse. For example, in Gainsborough, there is no record of almshouses but Lord Burgh's charity paid four poor bedesmen whose duty was to sweep Lord Street which led up to the old manor house. In Scothern there were no almshouses but Robert Grantham left £16 per annum by his will of 1616 for 'ten most poor, aged and impotent men of Scothern, Dunholme or Sudbrooke .....certain beadsmen [sic], poor aged creatures' who were to be present at a service in Dunholme church twice yearly when the preacher was 'required to remember and publish this pious and charitable use and disposition'. They would then receive their stipend and (on All Saints' day) a gown of strong cloth.

By various means the poor were dealt with, or disposed of, but a small group of virtuous (later they would be called respectable) poor, mostly widows, emerged. These blameless, impoverished persons could be helped by the building of almshouses. At the same time their benefactors might be revered and their names perpetuated.

Numerous almshouses were founded during the seventeenth century - Alford 1668; Ashby cum Fenby in 1641; Belton (near Grantham) 1659; Burton by Lincoln 1651 - and many others. With the advent of Protestantism and the abolition of chantries in the previous century bequests for the promotion of souls were impossible but bequests, with a name possibly inscribed in stone on a building, (Revd Francis Burton of Grimoldby) could and were left by those with the welfare of the poor at heart. One benefactor, in 1663, went so far as to compel inmates to wear a badge with the testator's name on the sleeve (Kirton in Holland).

Sometimes a group or groups of almshouses in a town could be administered under one body as in the case of Spalding. Spalding is a town with the

Alice, wife of Sir John Brownlow, founded a Bedehouse for six poor women at Belton near Grantham in 1659. It was rebuilt in 1827 with "Piae senectae domus" (a home for the pious and elderly) inscribed above the gateway. After the Second World War, the almshouse was purchased by the National Trust and converted to two apartments which are still used as almshouses.

administration of charities, including almshouses, well documented as they were dealt with by a continuous collection of worthies known as the Town Husbands. [Husbandry is in the sense of managing resources thriftily] This was an arrangement not uncommon in English small towns but it is unique in that it still survives here. Spalding Town Husbands have existed for four centuries and in 1665 the term 'Town Husbands' was first used to describe the Feoffees of Gamlyn's Almshouses (The trustees of charities were known as Feoffees). The vicar was always a Town Husband; the Headmaster of the Grammar School was another constant. In 1857 the Town Husbands resolved to appoint a medical man to the almshouses and thereafter a doctor nearly always appears as a member. Frequently sons followed fathers as Town Husbands. The picture is of sensible, educated men administering the local charities - the 'magistrate' class. They have been described as 'about twenty of the most influential inhabitants of the town, continued by self-selection upon the occurrence of vacancies'. Occasionally there was a hiccup in proceedings. By 1908 the Urban Council had representatives amongst the Town Husbands and they complained that they were treated as inferiors. Mr Hall, a member of the Urban District Council and a Town Husband, vented some spleen against his fellow members at a Special Meeting when reporters were present. He later apologised publicly. One of his allegations was that the Town Husbands 'attempted to enforce religious tests as a qualification for election'. He also stated that the estates were mismanaged and, as a result, the almspeople received 1/- per week each less than they were entitled to receive. In 1971 it was resolved to reduce the number of Husbands to nine from 25. Town Husbands did not include women in their ranks until 1979. This excellent body of people continue to work in the interests of the people of Spalding in a way which is remarkable in its continuity. The town comes under the umbrella of South Holland District Council yet the medieval structure of the Town Husbands still holds sway to the satisfaction of the inhabitants whose rates are not burdened by the existence of a Town Hall and mayor. The Town Husbands administer a large proportion of Spalding rented housing in the form of almshouses which are well maintained, the assets frequently invested in yet more new almshouses. In common with most other almshouse charities Spalding charges a maintenance rent which is paid or subsidised, in cases of need, by a state allowance thus a good income is assured. Many Spalding

The almshouses of Spalding are remarkable in that they were (and, uniquely, still are to this day) administered by 'the Town Husbands' a group of worthy Spalding men and (since 1979) women. Gamlyn's Almshouses have been managed by the Town Husbands since 1665. They were rebuilt in Gothic style (above) in 1844 with a crest showing three mallets above the door.

people prefer an almshouse to a council house and there is no shortage of applicants - the majority of new almshouse residents are previous council tenants.

Small almshouses built in the seventeenth century were vernacular in style and would often be of the local mud and stud construction with a brick chimney. An account dated 1672 for the bedehouses at Wrangle includes the following items: "*bricks to head the chimneys; bushell of lime to white the chimneys; thatcher; mason and a man; two men and a mare to make earth two days to rigg the beadhouse; John Kerby and his mare two days to flead the earth; John Lyon for temperinge the earth; for walling and wrighting the low house.*" This clearly gives a picture of the structure rising from the ground with the earth for the walls dug out on site. Thatching and nails appear regularly in accounts for maintenance and also small items such as (1722) 'paid for mending ye Bede windows 7d'. In 1725 there are notes about a new bakehouse built in place of an old hovel adjoining the bedehouse of the schoolmaster, 'for the mutual benefit of all singular and present and future member of the said Beadhouse...for baking and brewing'. In Wrangle in 1743 6lbs of nails, deals [wood] and bricks were purchased.

Kirkby Underwood bedehouse, founded 1638, was brick built. A description written in 1937 when the houses were in a poor state of repair states that the houses face due south with short wings at east and west forming a small sunny courtyard. At the west end there is a really beautiful ashlar chimney stack: 'They have had to take the top down but the stones are safe if re-erection is impossible.' The small courtyard tends to mirror the medieval plan although the buildings are in no way monastic here[3].

The traditional giver of alms, the church, could also assist the poor through a combination of education and housing. Sometimes these two aims were combined. In 1710 John Disney, a Presbyterian, reported to Bishop Wake that, in Lincoln, 120 poor children were taught by four poor clergymen's widows. These widows were given a house, rent paid, £10 per annum and a load of coals annually. In 1727, in Hemingby, a school and almshouses were built together and one of the almswomen received £4 annually for teaching young children. There are several other examples of schools and almshouses being linked such as King Edward VI's Bedehouses in Louth, the Fisher Almshouses in Bourne and the Cowley Charity houses in Donington.

Wrangle Almshouses (Alenson's Charity) created in 1555 was another case of the link between education and housing. A small soft leather-covered account and memorandum book[4] survives from the years 1671-1747 and gives an insight into this dual-purpose bequest. The schoolmaster apparently lived in one of the bedehouses; he was a figure of some little authority but he was answerable to the trustees who, if they disapproved of his actions, did not hesitate to admonish him. In 1721 a memorandum noted that William Longhorn, schoolmaster, was admonished a first time for not only being 'over rigorous to some of the children coming to ye said school' but likewise being 'negligent in ye performance of his Duty in teaching ye said Children'. The note was signed by Richard Baily, Vicar of Wrangle; Richard Kirke, Curate of Leake; two Wrangle churchwardens and two Leake churchwardens. Apparently the schoolmaster survived that little storm but in 1731 he was in a more serious situation as a petition was raised by members of the School Board and several inhabitants of Wrangle and Leake. He was accused of neglect and abuses. Longhorn resigned in 1733. Another master was taken that year and we gain a knowledge of what was taught in the agreement. He was 'to teach all persons who shall report to him being inhabitants of Wrangle and Leake, to teach English and Latin gratis'. He also had to teach catechism and officiate for the Parish Clerk if he were absent.

Troubles continued in Wrangle. Some ten years later, in 1743, John Allenson, schoolmaster, was admonished for 'neglect in teaching and unkind and barbarous usage of children'. This man lived in the bedehouses. He was not allowed to 'contract matrimony or frequent alehouses without leave or licence or become notoriously immoral'. He had to instruct persons in the church catechism and bring them duly and orderly to church as often as a bell shall be tolled for the purpose...' John Allenson signed this agreement in the book.

Teachers were not the only bedespeople to be admonished. In 1741 one John Tolle was taken to task for 'willfully refusing to deliver up his daughter to Christopher Jessop to whom she was put out by the parish and kept her at his own room in the Beadhouse where he is a member and under the heavy affliction of the small poxe to the very great detriment of the School thereto belonging'. John Tolle died in 1745.

Rose Margison received her first admonition in 1744 for 'wilfully harbouring a woman of ill fame and after various rebukes suffering her to lodge with her'. Lodgers were not permitted in Wrangle - nor was matrimony. In 1683 Robert Walsh of Leake, widower, was admitted to the Bedehouse instead of John Lyon 'who hath lately taken to him a wife thereby disabling himself for being any longer a Bedesman there'.

A rare glimpse into the lives of a couple of early beneficiaries of almshouses is provided by documents. It is unusual for poor people, such as the dwellers in almshouses were by definition, to leave records behind as far back as the seventeenth century. Probate inventories were generally for those with, at least, modest assets but there is one which tells of the worldly goods of Henry Richardson of Stamford described as beadsman. The document[5] records that its making is for 'paying his debt and legacies (if any such be) so far as the said goods and chattels will extend and as the law doth bind.' There were only two items listed: 'In the house bed and bedding £1; 4 pieces of old pewter 4s. 6d. Total £1. 4. 6d.' Through his scanty possessions Henry Richardson's name is known to us over three centuries later.

Another poor man, Nicholas Marckham of Gainsborough, also described as beadsman, had run up some debts before his death. There is a post-mortem administration account drawn up for him[6], apparently in order to settle the debts. It seems possible that he had needed care from the parish before his death as many of the debts are to men on behalf of their wives e.g. 'To Christopher Smith, his wife, 5s'. There is one payment owed to Gainsborough church for £1 (purpose unspecified) - this and several debts in shillings amount to £7.5.3d. Nicholas had purse, goods and chattels valued at £7.9.3d. so it would appear at first sight that he lived within his means. This he may have done but his death tipped him over the scales into debt in the grave. 'Funeral expenses and garb and singing' cost 5/- and the 'mortmaine' cost 3s.4d. The clerical expenses for drawing up the account were a hefty £1.3.4d. Mortmaine or mortmain

ALMSHOUSES AT REVESBY.

Joseph Banks, Esq., who died in 1727, left instructions by his will, that this House should be erected for a respectable man or woman of not less than 60 years of age.

The Owner of Revesby is required to provide £5 a year to the tenant of this Almshouse. The tenant is expected to go "to Church, on Sundays and Christmas Day, or any Public Feasts or Rejoicings appointed by Law," and is also expected not to remain away from "his or her room above a night in a month" without giving Notice thereof to the Chaplain of Revesby.

The tenant of this house is required to assist, if possible, any of the occupiers of the other nine Almshouses "when they are sick or under weakness or other infirmites."

The tenant may be removed "for plain misdemeanors, such as drunkenness, quarrelsomeness or other disorders, and also for not keeping his or her rooms clean, decent, and in good order."

There were usually rules governing the behaviour of the inmates of almshouses. This notice at Revesby makes it clear that church attendance is expected and absence from the almshouse, without leave, is not permitted. Drunkenness or untidiness could be grounds for eviction.

(French for dead hand) refers to land held by the church and payment for its use is recoverable after death.

Neat houses and neat old people, sometimes in uniform, came to form an attractive feature in many villages and towns. The benefits were usually good and practical. Apart from a roof over the head and clothing, fuel and cash were frequently provided and a little land for the able-bodied aged to cultivate. Sometimes deeds stipulated that the healthy old people were to nurse the more afflicted and occasionally servant care is mentioned when necessary as at the Carre Hospital in Sleaford. Bequests of material for gowns and cloaks were common. Nowadays, in a welfare state, benefits are also received in kind. For example many pensioners in almshouses are exempt from buying a television licence and paying Community Tax and water rates by almshouse trustees.

Most founders in earlier years had been landowners but a few exceptions began to appear. Matthew Humberston, who took his name from the village which he endowed with houses (1709), was the son of a foundling who had made good. Thomas Bell of Kingerby was a successful apothecary in London and left money to benefit and embellish his natal village (1675). Hopkins' Hospital, Stamford (1770) received contributions from the town Corporation and also from a company of comedians. Later Primitive Methodists, born poor boys, Samuel Ellis and James Davis were instrumental in the foundation of the Fishermen's Almshouses in Grimsby.

Several almshouses provided uniforms for their inmates and the buttons on coats and cloaks often depicted the founder's arms or mark, as in these examples from Carre's Hospital, Sleaford (above) and the Orme Bedehouses, Louth (below)

(Drawn by David Hopkins - Carre's Hospital buttons loaned courtesy of the Sleaford Museum Trust))

GAZETTEER

Almshouses founded 1550 – 1800

49. Addlethorpe: 3 miles west of Skegness – Bede-cottage bequeathed by **Samuel Mottram** of Addlethorpe Hall in 1710 - a residence for two poor people with half an acre of land adjoining for their use and two chaldrons of coal. Recipients should receive the sacrament in the parish church at Ingoldmells. The house is colour washed red brick with a pantile roof and 20th century gabled porches. (P)

50. Alford: West Street. (rebuilt 1870). In 1668 **Sir Robert Christopher** bequeathed £550 for building and endowing an almshouse for six poor women. The sum was subsequently augmented by Lord Harborough in 1716 with a yearly rent charge of £22. In 1870 the almshouses were rebuilt by the late Right Honourable Lady Mary Christopher-Nisbet-Hamilton and each inmate received a small sum weekly and bread. There is now a small maintenance contribution to pay. Four almshouses are available for couples or single people. Currently (2000) two of the houses stand empty. (S)

51. Ashby cum Fenby: 6 miles south of Grimsby. **Lady Frances Wray** erected, in her lifetime, almshouses for six poor men or women of Ashby or Barnoldby and six from Beckingham, Grainsby or Waithe. In 1641 her son Sir Christopher Wray endowed them with a yearly rent charge of £30. In 1825 a bill was filed on behalf of the almspeople as the land involved in the endowment changed hands. Judgement was given in 1829 that the new owners had to comply with the terms of the 1641 grant. The two Ashby almspeople had also the interest of £200 left by the Revd Woodthorpe Johnson M A vicar of Grainsby from 1844. The houses, which stand close to the church, have been repaired and altered over time. They are brick-built with pantiled roofs and consist of a terrace of four one-storey cottages each containing a bed-sitting room, kitchen and bathroom. People from Ashby and surrounding villages are eligible to occupy the houses but there is no shop and the bus service to Grimsby is sparse. A maintenance contribution is payable. (S)

52. **Bardney:** 7 miles south east of Lincoln. **Handcock's Hospital** was founded by the will of Peter Handcock dated 1708. A house for seven men and seven women was erected in 1712. The charity lapsed and by 1837 the provision for the inmates was as follows: nine inmates relieved by the parish and one by Greenwich Hospital. In 1837 the religious service had not been performed by the incumbent for several years due, he said, to 'total want of attendance'. He did, however, receive £10 p.a. from Lord Harrowby's steward for that duty as appointed by Handcock's will. Now the houses have been modified into six flats. The upper flats all have a stairlift provided and all residents are given a lifeline telephone. A small maintenance sub-scription is paid for the flats. Residents have to be 55 years or more and have a connection with Bardney or Southrey over a period of time. A land endowment of four acres in Bardney parish still provides income for the houses. (S)

Bardney: Handcock's Hospital, an almshouse for seven men and seven women, was built in 1712 by bequest of Peter Handcock. It was modified in the 20th century to form six flats for elderly people with a Bardney or Southrey connection.

53. **Barkston or Barkston le Willows:** 4 miles from Grantham. **Hickson's Almshouses** were built by bequest in his will of 1640 by Richard Hickson for six poor persons. He stipulated that they were to be built within twelve months of his death. The bequest was endowed with land in Rutland. Two ladies added £100 and £84 at an unknown date (pre 1837). The almsmen had to be 'accounted a proper object unless 60 years of age or more'. The six Bedehouses were re-built in 1839 in Belton estate style (by subscription) for poor persons. They were converted to three dwellings and modernised about 1970 for local people with genuine need, over 60 years of age. (S)

Barkston: Hickson's Almshouses were founded for six poor persons in 1640, and rebuilt in 1839 in 'Belton Estate' style. The accommodation was modernised and converted into three apartments in the 1970s.

54. **Barton on Humber:** a) **Holland's Almshouses** were four houses in Paradise Close. They were willed by Thomas Holland, fellmonger, (tanner) in 1669 for four poor women. In 1837 they were said to be in good repair and a Mr Johnston, then occupying Holland's house in Soutergate, paid the endowment properly as it was a condition of his purchase of the house. The houses no longer exist. (X)

55. **Barton on Humber**: b) In 1701 Christopher Benton bequeathed the **Chantry House**, north of Saint Mary's church, in Barton as an almshouse for the poor. In 1723 Thomas Johnson willed £20 to be placed out at interest for 'the use of the Poor of Barton'. This was laid out in the rebuilding of the house which was converted into a workhouse in 1749 and the overseers

afterwards spent about £200 of various charity moneys in enlarging it. In 1878 it was sold and the amount realised (£345.3.9d.) was invested in Consols (consolidated stock: government securities raised from various taxes), the dividends arising therefrom being applied by the overseers towards the charities. This building became the Poor House and is now demolished. (X)

56. Belton: near Grantham. Bedehouse for six poor women built in 1659 founded by Alice wife of Sir John Brownlow bart. whose portrait was in the bedehouse in 1905. Each inmate received £10 yearly at that date. The cottages form three sides of a rectangle. In 1827 it was rebuilt - *Piae Senectae Domus* was inscribed above the entrance gate. The thatch was replaced with slates and the roof raised at this date. The 1881 census gives Rebecca Foottet, 69, as a resident. Following World War II the building was bought by The National Trust and the six cottages were made into two. (S)

57. Benington: near Boston. Built in 1728 by the charity of **Mr William Porril** (died 1725). There were four bedehouses next to the church for two bedesmen and two bedeswomen who received 5/6d per week each in 1905. Originally three milk cows and three acres of pasture were given for the bedespeople and schoolmaster but *c.* 1840 it was found more beneficial to discontinue keeping cows and make an allowance instead. One poor bedesman turned out to be less than poor. James Rheson left a bequest to the church. He had left a will leaving all his worldly possessions to start a fund for a clock in the church tower. He declared he had 'nowt to leave' but 1100 half crowns (£137.50) were found in an old chest in the bedehouse. A report in *The Lincolnshire Echo* of 3rd November 1978. states that the trustees wanted to demolish the almshouses but were prevented by the Department of the Environment as they were listed buildings (brick with seven sash windows and pantiled roof). Then known as Porril and Cowell's Trust. Now (2000) the four houses are occupied by one couple and three single people who were formerly residents of Leverton or Benington. (S)

58. Boston: a) Boston Municipal Charities. **St John's Row**, which no longer exists, was, according to Pishey Thompson, mentioned in 1635 and 1640 when it contained ten tenements 'formerly used as pest houses'. There were sixteen houses in 1690. It was last mentioned in 1711 when it was directed that 'the almshouses there should be repaired'. The workhouse was built on this site *c.* 1730. (X)

59. Boston: b) **St Leonard's Hospital**, Hospital Bridge: The successor to St John's Hospital was sold by Boston Corporation to Alderman Barkham in 1623. The endowment of approximately 53 acres of land called the Leakes and £35 pa for ten bedesmen was dated 1765 and 1776. By 1872 the parish of Skirbeck was bound to keep the hospital in repair. The successor to this hospital still exists on the site but the old buildings are gone. (X)

60. Bourne: Now combined in one charity (Bourne United Charities) but based on two old foundations: a) **Fisher's Almshouses** in Water Lane were built by William Fisher in 1620, during his lifetime, for six poor women. The room in the house where he once lodged himself was to be used for a schoolmaster. The Charity Commissioners commented in 1837 that it was difficult to identify this room as there were only six rooms in the house. Each widow had a room and a coal house. (X)

61. Bourne: b) **Trollope's Almshouses**: William Trollope's will of 1636 bequeathed £30 per annum from rent in Weston to six poor men in several habitations. He proposed a convenient habitation to be built for them. The men were to be selected from poor, aged or decrepit men of Bourne. These two groups (Bourne a & b) were replaced by thirteen brick bungalows built in West Street in 1931. They house twelve residents (six men and six women) and a warden. (S)

62. Branston: 4 miles southeast of Lincoln. **Mere Hospital** was re-founded in 1553. The warden and his servant were to have one honest chamber with a chimney and stable for two horses and litter for same while the warden was resident. There was a chapel and the warden was to choose three poor men as residents and provide them with meat, drink, fuel, bedding, clothes and other necessities and find yearly one honest priest to maintain divine service there at all times. There is now nothing to be seen but humps and bumps in the field in front of Mere Hall. (X)

63. Burton by Lincoln: Founded in 1712 by Sir J Monson bart. KGP, MP, rebuilt in 1879 by Viscount Oxenbridge for eight poor widows of the parishes of Burton, Broxholme and N and S Carlton who each received 3/4d per month (1905). They have also divided amongst them an annuity of £5 left in 1712 by Edward Monson esq. of Burton. The houses are now let to people in need, not necessarily elderly people although the elderly would have precedence over others. (P)

64. Cockerington St Mary (North Cockerington): 4 miles northeast of Louth. **Scroope's Almshouse** was bequeathed by Sir Jarvis Scroope in 1670. He wished the almshouse to be repaired 'for ever' and any 'surplusage' from the endowment to be bestowed on the poor on Plough Monday yearly. The almshouses were rebuilt in 1811 by Mr S T Scrope. By 1837 the payment of 2/6d weekly was supplemented from the Poor Rates. The present building was built in 1888. It was a single storey range consisting of four houses in brick and slate. In 1968 the houses were all empty; there was a kitchen with range and side oven and stone sink. The water supply was an outside tap and there was an earth closet and coal-house for each house. The trustees consulted with the Charity Commissioners and the decision was made to sell the houses and enter the proceeds into the Scroope Charity for distribution to needy people in various forms. The houses are now owned privately and converted into one bungalow. (P)

65. Croft: 2 miles north of Wainfleet. Two cottages together with three acres of land were left in 1585 by **John Drope** for two poor families, the trustees being the vicar and churchwardens, the families being elected for life. A further three homes were erected in 1908 (The Rookery). All are now gone, demolished in the 1950s. John Drope's Charity is administered by the Parish Council and a sum of money is divided between deserving elderly inhabitants of Croft each Christmas. (X)

66. Denton: near Grantham. In 1786 **William Welby** gave by deed a house (already existing, built in 1653) for six poor widows and a rent-charge, £18.12s for its support. In 1837 it was described as being situated near the Park with *1653* and *WW* inscribed on it. At that date it held three widows and three widowers. Pevsner described it as 'what may well be the most delightful almshouses in England'. They were built in local ironstone with Dutch gables and had six hearths (17th century Hearth Tax records). In the early 1960s they were still in good repair but by 1967 some dereliction was apparent. In 1980 a repairs order was served by South Kesteven District Council on Sir Bruno Welby and the Welby Estate who, in defiance of the order, had the Grade 2* listed almshouses demolished. The Society for Preservation of Ancient Buildings prosecuted Sir Bruno and, in March 1981, he was fined £1,000 and ordered to pay £2,000 costs for unauthorised demolition. The cost to Sir Bruno was low as he achieved his aim of ridding his park of a public attraction and the almshouses are no more. (X)

67. Denton: Blyth Cottages Charity. The charity was founded by an endowment of 1696 by John Blyth of Shoxton, Orson of Whitsundine, Rutland and Elizabeth King of Denton. A cottage in Harlaxton with grazing for three sheep and nine cows provided money by rental for maintenance of the first almshouse. Presumably this first building was a thatched mud and stud cottage as a document of 1794 suggest that it be pulled down and replaced with a 'good and substantial one, of similar dimensions, to be covered with good tiles. There are now two rows of brick almshouses which are run by trustees in conjunction with a Housing Association. Residents are local people when possible. It seems likely that the present houses stand on a plot of land given by an unknown donor to the church and churchwardens at enclosure in exchange for a house belonging to the poor of the parish. (S)

68. Donington: 11 miles southwest of Boston. **Cowley's Charity** was formed by the will of Thomas Cowley, proved in 1726. Twelve almshouses were to be built for ten poor men and women who through age or sickness or any other misfortune were incapable of providing for themselves. They were to have 2/- per week each and half a chaldron of coals and a gown not exceeding 20/- in value yearly. Land was endowed for the purpose and a large addition was made to this charity at the enclosure of the fens. The charity document was long and detailed and encompassed several matters including the foundation of a school. The Cowley School exists but it seems the almshouses were never built. (X)

69. Fosdyke: near Holbeach. Ten brick almshouses known as **Middlecott's Hospital**. Pevsner says built in 1625 by Sir Thomas Middlecott; Kelly's (1905) says Sir

Fosdyke: Middlecott's Hospital was founded in the early seventeenth century for a master and ten poor people of good name and repute. The building is too remote for today's elderly people and was sold in the late 1970s, the proceeds being used to build four modern bungalows in more convenient locations. Middlecott's Hospital has now been converted to form a group of very pleasant private dwellings.

Thomas Middlecott's almshouse founded c. 1800 for the poor of Fosdyke and Algarkirk. This must be wrong as the Charity Commissioners of 1837 described the bedehouse as the 1658 building of brick and thatch insured with the Sun Fire Office for £500. Sir Thomas Middlecott procured in his lifetime an Act of Parliament for the erecting of a hospital for a master and ten poor people to be elected and chosen of the poor and impotent, either bachelor or maid, widower or widow of good name and repute of the age [at least] of forty years. Inmates were to receive 8d per week for ever and a cloak containing four yards and a load of turf and a half chaldron of sea coals. Between 1720 and 1837 the master's office fell into disuse. This charity was disadvantaged by the Enclosure of 1812-13 as the land-holding, which produced rent, was lessened by 3 acres 1 rood 25 perches. In 1837 the Charity Commissioners found that, for many years, only one man and nine women were appointed; they pointed out to the trustees that this was not correct. At that date trustees met annually on Good Friday to audit and examine and an entertainment was provided for trustees, bedespeople and tenants. The charity was endowed with 98 acres of land producing £204 yearly in 1905. The building held ten inmates of either sex - four from Fosdyke and six from Algarkirk. They received £13.13s per annum in 1905. The houses are now privately owned. Two brick bungalows were built in Fosdyke and two in Algarkirk which were opened on 21st November, 1981. The money for these new almshouses was raised partly from the sale of the old hospital and partly from land in the original bequest. Present residents must be single, can be male or female and resident in Fosdyke or Algarkirk. They live rent-free and all decorating and maintenance is provided for them. (P)

70. Freiston: (near Boston). **Thomas Truesdale's Charity**: In 1694 Truesdale gave one cottage and yard near the church and also a cottage and yard in Freiston Crave (now Scrave) End for use of the poor for ever. (X)

71. Freiston: (near Boston). An indenture of 1595 made between Simon Clarke yeoman and Richard Dowse and 13 others granted an annuity to four poor people of £8 and any overplus should be distributed to the pensioners in fuel. This was continued until 1756 from which date trustees were elected at a public vestry and an amount distributed to four poor infirm unmarried people. The trustees built two bungalows in 1926 and these were let at a nominal rent to old people. This and several other small charities were revised by the Charity Commissioners in 1953 and amalgamated. The site of the old cottages at Church End Frieston was sold to the Rural District Council who agreed to build six bungalows for old people. Later (circa 1970s) the trustees were able to build four brick bungalows from the fund and these are allotted generally to widows of the parish. (S)

72. Freiston: (near Boston). **Alexander Holland's cottages** – these were given in 1604 with garthstead and half an acre. The cottage had fallen into decay by 1828. Two new cottages, each containing four rooms, were erected on the site at a cost of £120 and let for £5 each per annum to two widows. There is no trace of them now. (X)

73. Glentworth: near Kirton in Lindsey. Three tenements situated in the churchyard and repaired as occasion requires by Lord Scarbrough (1937) and occupied by one man and two women commonly called Glentworth pensioners. Formerly there were six pensioners who received each £2 per annum but now three who have £4 each and the tenement free. Also nine bushels of coal per annum and, every third or fourth year, nine yards of blue cloth. This charity is supposed to have been founded by the Wray family. Parliamentary Returns of 1786 state that a person unknown built a house for six poor widows, rent free and cloth for a gown every other year worth 13/- apiece and the owner of the manor and lordship of Glentworth was liable to maintain tenements and pay pensioners. Sir Christopher Wray, the Lord Chief Justice, in his will dated 30th July, 1589, enjoined his son William and heirs or assigns to maintain six poor persons of honest conversation and religion in the almshouses at Glentworth, built by him, with 10d each per week, a gown yearly and three loads of ashwood and three loads of turf, that the said poor people should have dinner every Sunday in Glentworth Hall, if able to come thither, or else every one a 1d loaf of bread...if his son or heirs should default he empowered the Dean and Chapter of Lincoln to distrain yearly on tenants for money, wood etc. and also for £3 monthly. The houses still exist but are no longer almshouses. (P)

74. Gosberton: a) 6 miles northwest of Spalding. '**Widow's Row**' consisted of eight small terraced cottages in Salem Street which were bequeathed by Henry Gate in 1707. The row was brick-built and, at least in latter years, roofed with pantiles although the pitch would suggest that it was once thatched. The tiny dwellings consisted of a bed-sitting room and a scullery. As late as 1977, when the row was demolished, there were still no basic modern facilities, not even a sink, although there was one electric point each and a cold water tap. Four earth closets still served the eight houses. Originally the half acre of garden bestowed contained a well for the use of residents. Money from the bequest is now paid to pensioners at Christmas and housing for the elderly is provided by South Holland Council who bought the tenements. They have been replaced by houses administered by the Longhurst Housing Association. (X)

75. Gosberton: b) **2-16 Church Street**. Money was bequeathed in the will of Sarah Nelsey in 1750 and the houses were eventually built in 1792. They consisted of a brick terrace of two-storey cottages. These were sold in 1973 to H Moore and Son who built private houses on the site. The proceeds were incorporated in the Gosberton Relief in Need Fund. (X)

76. Grantham: Grantham Almshouse Charity. Thomas Hurst DD in 1671 gave almshouses adjoining the church of Saint Wulfram for eight poor widows rent free. **Hurst's Almshouses** (Church Street) benefited by two prior wills of 1597 (when there was a bequest by Francis Trigg) and another bequest by Anthony Acomes in 1640. Later Arabella Langwith left money for the poor in 1857. All this was redirected in 1860 - Langwith's for maintenance of widows in Hurst's almshouses and the other for repairs to the houses and paying the six senior almspersons a sum not exceeding 6/- nor less than 3/6d per week). (X)

77. Grimoldby: near Louth. Revd Francis Burton left by will in 1780 a new brick and tiled house which cost £50. On the wall was an inscription: *Hanc beneficio pauperum F Burton condidit 1780*. By 1857 it was in use as a Poor House by the parish. (X)

78. Haxey: Isle of Axholme. **Farmery's Almshouses**, Low Street, were bequeathed by the will of Mrs Jane Farmery in 1723. There were four tenements already built and two more directed to be built. A seventh tenement was added some 100 years later by the parish. The 1881 census returns give Rebeka Graves, 68, a labourer's widow as resident in an almshouse. By 1905 there is no mention of almshouses. They are said to have been demolished within living memory (from 2001). (X)

Hemingby: A terraced row of four cottage almshouses and a school were erected in 1727 by Jane Dymoke, who included an endowment in her will to enable the poor children of the parish to be taught to read, write and spin and card wool. The row consists of six bays and it is thought that one cottage could have been the schoolmaster's house and one the school. The houses are traditionally placed adjacent to the churchyard and still function as almshouses although now modernised and converted to three residences.

79. Hemingby: near Horncastle. Almshouses in Church Walk. Five cottage almshouses were erected in the year 1727 by **Jane Dymoke**. Kelly's (1905) refers to four almshouses (no date) with an endowment of £6 yearly and 2 tons of coal each for four poor widows inhabitants of the county of Lincoln. Pevsner refers to a school and hospital. Income for the charity is derived from land at Woodhall and Asterby and the house and farm occupied by the schoolmaster, worth upwards of £40 a year. The houses, now three in number, still exist and function using income from the original endowment but the land is now at Poolham, a hamlet near Horncastle. White's (1856) says that four almswomen receive 2/3d weekly with an allowance of fuel. One of them receives an extra sum of £4 per annum for teaching a number of young children. A plaque on the houses reads: *This Hospital and School were erected in the year 1727 by Jane Dymoke Widow of the Hon Charles Dymoke of Scrivelsby Esq Champion of England and endowed by her with a yearly salary to a School Master and Mistress for teaching the poor children in the parish of Hemingby to read write and spin and card wool.* The trustees are currently (2001) business men, farmers and the vicar. There are now no rules or religious stipulations attached to residence but almspeople must get on well together. Within living memory there were tools provided for tilling the land. The buildings (now three cottages) are listed Grade II. (S)

80. Humberston: 5 miles southeast of Grimsby. Pevsner says that Robert Adams made designs for houses which were not executed. Matthew Humberston bequeathed money in 1709 for, among other things, the erection and endowment of almshouses which were to be 'a fit habitation for six poor men or women...as the trustees....shall think proper objects'. Attendance at church was compulsory every Lord's day and 'every other day appointed for God's worship'. Humberston was the son of a foundling who had made good. More than a century elapsed between the bequest and the establishment of a charity. The almshouses were built in 1821. They were for six poor men or women of the parish of Humberston. There was a long and expensive litigation between Lord Carrington and the Trustees culminating in a new scheme in 1850 for the school and almshouses. Seventeen new Trustees were appointed. By 1905 the charity was administered by the Lord of the Manor, the vicar and two churchwardens plus two people elected by the vestry of Humberston. Annuities were set apart for the almshouses which contained six inmates who received 6/- per week. Each person was required to attend the Parish Church each Sunday and other appointed days if physically able. Neglect of this rule or misconduct could lead to a person's removal from the almshouses. The charity is now called **The Humberston Almshouse Foundation**. (S)

81. Irnham: 2 miles northeast of Corby Glen and 10 miles southeast of Grantham. Six stone almshouses near the castle gateway were built in 1712 by John Thimbleby. White's (1856) mentions that John Thimbleby esq. in 1712 charged the manor of Irnham 4/- a week each and firing for four poor widows of the Roman Catholic faith. The 1881 census states that Charles Hockley, aged 32, agricultural labourer was a resident in an almshouse so presumably, at this date, they were not all used for their original purpose. The buildings were restored and modernised in 1985. (S)

Irnham: Six stone almshouses were built in 1712 by John Thimbleby – restored and modernised in 1985.

82. Kingerby: 5 miles northwest of Market Rasen. A row of six almshouses west of the church, founded in 1675 and rebuilt in the early nineteenth century. Foundation and endowment by Thomas Bell who left £100 for the purpose. **Thomas Bell** was an apothecary of London who was born in Kingerby. There was a dispute over the payment in 1810 when Thomas Bell's heir, Isabella Peacock refused to pay the amount yearly produced by the endowment. It was taken to court and Peacock was ordered to pay the full amount, to defray the court costs and to repair the almshouses. The cottages were dismantled and rebuilt in 1994/5. Before this renovation the houses had become semi-derelict and one cottage has been used as a coal store with separate heaps of coal for each resident, while another was used as a communal washhouse. (S)

Kingerby: Six almshouses were founded in 1675 and rebuilt in the early 1800s. By the late twentieth century they had become very dilapidated and in 1994/95 they were taken down and rebuilt. This photograph of the rebuilding shows that only the chimney stacks were retained. *(Photo: R. Russell)*

83. Kirkby Underwood: 5 miles north of Bourne. This endowment reflects the role of women at the time of foundation in 1638. It was made by the will of Richard Brownlow for almshouses for six almsmen and one almswoman to attend the men and wash their linen and keep their lodgings sweet and clean. Brownlow enjoined his heirs to, 'Place none in the almshouse that are of ill life or behaviour or able to get their living by labour.' The estate was sold to Sir Gilbert Heathcote by the heirs of Brownlow in 1714. The Charity Commissioners noted, in 1837, that the houses had rarely been used for the purpose for which they were intended since 1714, being used instead for old servants and dependents. Archive correspondence of 1752/3 indicates that the bedehouses were a burden to administrators[7]. 'I was lately at Kirkby and the tenant complained much of the trouble he had in paying the beadmen and that he would not do it any longer. As I am concerned for Sir John, who I understand is only obliged to pay £59.3s: - I am at a loss how that can be executed for the future. Formerly I am told in Mr Triggs' time when he was steward to both the familys he now and then put in a man of Kirkby, Rippingale or Haconby and that they, according to the donor's will, presided there which was a convenience to the parish of Kirkby and Rippingale and, for that small help of an old man now and then, the principal tenant was willing to take the trouble - but now it is otherwise...I wish you would look into ye donor's will where you will find residence to strongly injoined that I can't help thinking in ye way it is now would be thought perverted and I am told that their [sic] is no covenant to pay the alms in the way it has been but Sir John may pay it in one sum to Lord Tyrconnel or to whom he shall appoint.' A letter of reply exists in which Lord Tyrconnel's agent, Valentine Haseldine, agrees that payment can be made twice yearly[8]. He mentions that Lord T has no copy of the donor's will. He also mentions that the almsmen are liable to be turned out ...'there is always a chance to oblige 'em to reside where my Lord (or Donor) orders 'em.' The final letter on the subject (not known to whom) from Haseldine is dated January 1753: '...the almsmen at Kirkby about whose residence my Lord will not take further advice: tho' it is, in general, considered as a sort of banishment to remove poor helpless men from their friends and acquaintance at a time when they most want their assistance; and to a place they are strangers to; with very indifferent accommodation, especially in illness; notwithstanding the best help that a poor old nurse can give 'em.' The letter goes on to say that the donor had lived near the bedehouses and could watch the bedesmen attend church - but now things were different. However, he concedes that the cottages would give 'an opportunity of providing for his own tenants and superannuated, infirm servants etc[9].' By 1837 they were described as being occupied by any poor people who could get possession. Early 20th century photographs show a resident standing at the gate of dilapidated cottages. There were five cottages in an E shape; four were of brick with Colley Weston tiles and the fifth was mud and stud. The houses were maintained by the levy of a 'tax' on certain local farms. This was known as a 'tithe' although it cannot have been a tithe in the normal sense of the word *i.e.* a payment to the established church or an impropriator. After the houses were demolished the 'tithe' was paid to the Brownlow estate which used it to maintain the almshouses at Barkston which were then used for retired estate workers. The cottages were demolished in 1939 after being condemned by Kesteven County Council. Apparently the oak beams were removed but there was some difficulty over access to the rest of the demolished materials. All was finally levelled and cleared. Two farms, Manor Farm and Grange Farm, (Wood and Green families in 2001) still make the payment known as 'tithe' locally and this money is paid through the Brownlow estate (now National Trust property) and returned to the Kirkby Parish Council who distribute it to pensioners in the village. (X)

84. Kirton in Holland: (4 miles from Boston): **Robert Hunt houses** administered by Kirton United Charities who also administer the later John Speak almshouses. The Hunt houses were founded in 1663 when the founder left 6/- per month to the senior inmate and 4/8d per month to the others – plus a gown and half a chaldron of coals annually. Inmates received on admittance one good grey cloth gown with a badge of the testator's name on the sleeve. In 1856 there were almshouses for four poor women built on the west side of the church 'near unto the Ash Tree'. Around 1974 they were renovated into two dwellings standing north of the Fire Station in Willington Road. They are of red brick with modern pantiles. There is an inscription: RAH 1664. (S)

85. Langton by Horncastle: brick-built in 1690 in Artisan Mannerist style - now derelict. Two almshouses for poor women were founded in 1690 by the **Revd Willoughby West** who left a farmhouse and land let at £23 per annum in 1905 when each almsperson received 3/- weekly and coals. Now called Langton United Charities. It is intended to renovate these cottages. No-one lives there at present (2000). (P)

86. Louth: King Edward VI's Hospital or bedehouse - Gospel Gate: The foundation dates from 1551 and is linked to the foundation of Edward VI's Grammar School. It was originally called Our Lady Bede House as the land of the endowment had formerly belonged to St Mary's Guild of Louth before the guilds were discontinued. The hospital was for twelve poor people. The premises formed part of the school edifice, occupying the ground floor. Shares from the endowment to the sum of 2/- per quarter were paid to bedespeople in 1837. A new school and bedehouses were built on the old

Market Rasen: St Poll Hospital, founded by Sir George St Poll in 1612, was originally for eight 'indigent men', although only five lived within the Hospital. The building is still an almshouse and is now divided into four cottages.

site in Schoolhouse Lane from designs by Fowler. In 1872 twelve poor people living there received 5/- per week each. The houses are now occupied by women. (S)

87. Market Rasen: **St Poll Hospital** founded in 1612 by Sir George St Poll of Snarford for eight indigent men, five of whom resided in the hospital. He bequeathed £200 for the erection of the buildings and £120 for land at Tealby (to be used for income). The four cottages, of stone and brick with a slate roof are inscribed: *Jesus Christ The Same Yesterday Today and Forever These Almshouses were founded by George St Pole Kt & Bart AD 1612.* His widow, Frances, Countess Dowager of Warwick, had an indenture made in 1626 with further directions. These included the condition that the choice of inmates should be in the sole right of the Lord of the Manor of Snarford provided that his name should be St Paul or else Sir John Wray or his heirs - providing they be lords or owners of Glentworth. Inmates should be from Snarford, Snelland, Faldingworth, Legsby and Market Rasen. The endowment seems to have been complicated e.g. in 1837, land in Riseholme that was involved in the arrangement became the property of Lord Brownlow - who continued to pay 40/- per annum. 15 acres in Buslingthorpe came into the ownership of Charter-house but the cut of hay from Lady Day to Midsummer fell to the Trust and was paid by the Charter-house estates - £71.4s in 1837. Residents were generally bachelors or widowers but, in 1837, a poor married man named Martin from Snarford, became a bedesman of the hospital although 'an old married man' in disabled circumstances. With the addition of other lands the trustees in 1905 were able to give residents £5.9s yearly and £4.11s to the three non-residents plus a bonus at Christmas of coal and clothes. The houses stand in Caistor Road (two are currently empty - 2000). Residence qualifications are generally liberal. The conditions state that applicants should live in the area and have a Christian background. Expulsion can result in cases of 'insobriety, insubordination, breech of regulations and immoral or improper conduct'. This has never happened in living memory. There is now no land endowment the money being all invested. Residents pay a contribution towards rent and their Council Tax and television licence is paid (if applicable).

Maintenance is carried out including lawn mowing. (S)

88. Potterhanworth: Foundation date not known but the **Culfrey Land Charity** existed in 1776 when the village was enclosed. It owned four cottages which were demolished in 1965 and a thatched, stone cottage, the Culfrey Cottage in Moor Lane which was left to the village for the use of the oldest poor man. Now there are two new bungalows, built 1972, in the Garth for retired parishioners. There was a condition attached to the old cottage that the occupant rang the church bell, known as the Culfrey Bell, at 7.00 pm each evening during winter to guide travellers. There was a tradition that the founder of the charity (name unknown) had been led to the village on a stormy winter evening by the sound of the bell and the endowment was his expression of thanks. This cottage was burnt down in 1931. The present Culfrey bell was cast by Taylors of Loughborough in 1897 and bears the inscription: *The old order changeth yielding place to new and God fulfils himself in many ways lest one good custom should corrupt the world.* Another village with a similar bell ringing tradition is Harlaxton. In this case, however, there is no known connection with an almshouse but the Harlaxton bell-ringer had the use of a field called Day Bell Close as recompense for his labour. The Harlaxton bell was rung at 8.00 pm each evening until the 1960s and at one time it was also rung at 4.00 am each morning. (X)

89. Revesby: between Horncastle and Boston. **Banks' Almshouses** were bequeathed by the will of Sir Joseph Banks (dated 1726) for ten poor decayed farmers come to poverty by loss of cattle or other inevitable accidents and not by idleness, drunkenness or other extravagance. Widows were also to be admitted. The houses were to be built on Revesby Green. Such as were able, were to help the heir or his family to get his hay in for 14 days every hay time. The almshouses were demolished in the 1980s and rebuilt in the same style, with slate roofs, as five dwellings on one level. At the time of demolition the following framed notice was hung in one of the houses: *Almshouses at*

Revesby: Sir Joseph Banks founded almshouses on the Green at Revesby for "ten poor decayed farmers come to poverty by loss of cattle or other inevitable accidents ..." The original almshouses were demolished in 1970 and rebuilt in the same style as five dwellings.

Revesby. Joseph Banks Esq., who died in 1727, left instructions by his will, that this House should be erected for a respectable man or woman of not less than 60 years of age. The Owner of Revesby is required to provide £5 a year to the tenant of this Almshouse. The tenant is expected to go "to Church, on Sundays and Christmas Day, or any Public Feasts or Rejoicings appointed by Law," and is also expected not to remain away from "his or her room above a night in a month" without giving Notice thereof to the Chaplain of Revesby. The tenant of this house is required to assist, if possible, any of the occupiers of the other nine Almshouses "when they are sick or under weakness or other infirmites." [sic] The tenant may be removed "for plain misdemeanors, such as drunkenness, quarrelsomeness or other disorders, and also for not keeping his or her rooms clean, decent, and in good order." The houses are maintained by The Joseph Banks' Almshouse Trust and tenants now pay a modest rent. Applicants must have lived in the county for a long time. There are no unusual rules of tenancy nowadays. (S)

90. Ruskington: near Sleaford. The almshouse was built as directed in the will of **Lady Anne Hodgson**, 1719, and the house was to contain 'all conveniences' for three poor women. Any woman who did not behave properly or neglected or refused to go to church was to be removed. In 1837 it was described as a low building with three rooms. The houses no longer exist and this charity is now concerned with education. (X)

Sleaford: Carre's Hospital in Eastgate, founded in 1636, was re-fronted in Tudor style by architect Charles Kirk in the 1830s/40s. The chapel at the centre has a large Perpendicular style window and a pointed bell gable.

91. Saltfleetby All Saints: In 1785 Revd Montague Chomeley DD left money for almshouses for four poor women. No trace can now be found of this charity. (X)

92. Sleaford: **Carre's Hospital** was bequeathed by the will of Robert Carre dated 1636. It was to be erected 'over against the church' and was described as a neat stone building. Twelve poor men with a woman, or manservant, to attend on them. About 1836

Sleaford: Carre's Hospital in Northgate was founded in 1636 and was rebuilt by Charles Kirk in 1857.

the Eastgate hospital was given a new Tudor-style front. A chapel was built in the grounds circa 1830. The Northgate hospital was rebuilt at a slightly later date (mid-Victorian). In 1872 the number of almspeople had been increased to 18 and they received 10/- per week, 1½ tons of coal per annum and a blue cloak. (S)

93. Spalding: a) **Town Husbands' Charity** incorporating: **Gamlyn's Almshouses** founded by Sir John Gamlyn, who died in 1591, for 34 men and women. There were six almshouses to the north of Church Street built in 1623. These were first rebuilt in 1751 by the Town Husbands. In 1763 three more almshouses were built. They were rebuilt in 1844 in Gothic style as a square in Church Street. There were 17 dwellings for 34 almspeople - males to west; females to east; couples in centre. The design was by a Mr Mitchell of Sheffield who won the contract by competition. The cost was £2,500 and the builders were Sharman, Sharp and Dawson. Each inmate received 3/6d weekly and one ton of coals yearly in 1905. Demolition of Gamlyn's almshouses was refused by the Planning Committee. It was noted that there was a conflict of comfort versus appearance. These houses are now in the care of the Council and are no longer almshouses. (P)

Spalding: Sir John Gamlyn founded six almshouses in Church Street in 1623; they were rebuilt and extended during the eighteenth century and reconstructed in their present, Gothic style in 1844.

94. Spalding: b) **Mrs E Sparke's**: eight almshouses were built in Double Street in 1717. Almshouses for six widows rebuilt in 1812. In 1836 Town Husbands' records mention four almshouses for five widows in Double Street. Each inmate received 3/6d weekly in 1905. There is no record of land for endowment of this charity but there is a record of the first almshouse being pulled down for widening the river in 1775 and £48.1s paid for the same and carried into the general account. These houses no longer stand. (X)

95. Spalding: c) **Charity of William Warrell**. He left his house on the Harrington House site, now Broad Street Car Park to the Town Husbands for the use of two widows in 1697. These houses no longer stand. (X)

96. Spalding: d) Tenements for eight poor widows were re-established in Double Street. **Lot Mael** collected funds and gave land in 1708 which was administered by the Town Husbands. These houses no longer stand. (X)

97. Spalding: e) **Willesby Almshouses**: cottage beside church porch. In 1630 this was inhabited by two old men. One almshouse is mention in a document of 1592 which is signed by William Willesby who lived in what is now the White Horse. The situation was later described as 'very inconvenient in Churchyard without back premises'. In 1668 a dwelling described as 'Shambles' was built behind the Town Hall. They were rebuilt in 1806 for four almspeople. In 1829 a Miss Johnson gave money for almspeople here. In 1885 these almshouses were closed. They are now demolished. (X)

98. Stamford: **Stamford Municipal Almshouse Charities** incorporates several foundations: a) **Snowden's almshouses**, Scotgate, adjoining Truesdale's, were founded in 1604 by Richard Snowden, Minister of the Church

Stamford: Snowden's Almshouses on Scotgate were founded in 1604 and rebuilt in 1822 to house eight poor, aged widows. (Photo: D Peall)

Stamford: Truesdale's Almshouse, adjoining Snowden's, on Scotgate, was founded in 1700 and rebuilt in 1833. (Photo: D Peall)

Stamford: Hopkins Hospital: founded by John Hopkins, Mayor of Stamford in 1770. Built in Gothic style with a castellated parapet.

of St John, and rebuilt in 1822 at a cost of £450 for eight poor aged widows, each of whom received 6/- weekly in 1905 plus other distributions half-yearly. Situated in Scotgate, they are single storey, Tudor Gothic, bed sitting rooms. The red brick chimneystacks were added in 1877. Further bequests to this charity were made by Mrs Mary Torkington who died in 1763 and John Warrington, gent who died in 1806. At present (2002) this building is empty but it seems likely that it will be let as an architect's office. Derek Gladman, chairman of Stamford Almshouse Charities, was reported in the press as saying that advertisements for new residents had failed to bring in applications so it was decided to lease the building for the time being. South Kesteven District Council's planning committee have approved the change of use. (P)

99. Stamford: b) **Truesdale's almshouses**, Scotgate, were founded in 1700 by Thomas Truesdale, who was an attorney with an extensive practice, and were re-erected in 1833 at a cost of £2,900. The architect was George Basevi. Pevsner says, 'a nice interplay of gables, pinnacles and octagonal chimneyshafts; ornate barbed quatrefoils in the gables; narrow street front with a central archway; behind, two long ranges of almshouses facing each other across a courtyard.' These houses have been modernised and are still in use. Shelter, food and clothing were afforded to sixteen aged poor of the parishes of St John and All Saints. Included in the rules were: 1) *Every person not hindered by sickness shall attend the Church of All Saints in gown and behave reverently;* 3) *No person to presume to be out after 9 at night;* 5) *Avoid brawling, quarrelling, swearing and drunkenness;* 7) *No person to hire himself as a Tapster or servant on fairs, markets - or any occasion;* 8) *Wives, if they visit, to avoid clamorous scolding and reproachful language.* Accommodation is for over-60s, single, divorced or widowed. An inscription reads: *This hospital was rebuilt and enlarged AD 1835 and 1843 under the direction of James Torkington, gent, James Hurst esq., T C Arnold MD Trustees. (S)*

100.Stamford: c) **All Saints Callis**: of unknown origin mentioned in Charity Commissioners' report and White's (1856). At that date it was described as a decayed old building at the corner of the Sheep-market containing rooms for seven poor aged women. Some of the endowment was from Henry Fryer. **Fryer's Callis** now stands on Kettering Road. This building was designed by George Basevi in 1832. [see Gazetter No. 178] (X)

101.Stamford: d) **Hopkin's Hospital**, St Peter's Street, (bed-sitting rooms) founded by subscription in 1770 during the mayoralty of a Mr John Hopkins. Mr Hopkins himself contributed as did the Corporation. The third significant contribution came from a performance by Mr Whitley's company of comedians. The cost of the building was £365. Later others also subscribed towards the upkeep. In 1856 it had rooms for eight poor people who had 2/8d each per week. Endowments included one from Henry Fryer and another from Mrs Rebecca Chamberlain who died in 1797. This lady also left bequests to Williamson's, All Saints' Callis and St John's Callis (Snowden's). Built in Gothic style; two blind windows to preserve symmetry; castellated parapet with openwork pinnacles; arms of Stamford. Subsidiary small units run by by the same trustees are **Austin Friars** and **Fryer's Callis Almshouses**, in Woolthorpe Road. (S)

102.Stamford: e) **Lord Burghley's Bede Houses**, Station Road, founded in 1597 for twelve poor old men of St Martin's parish and a warden. They received about 6/- per week in 1856 and a yearly clothing allowance and faggot wood. Now accommodation for local people of retirement age who do not own a house. The original buildings are still in use as almshouses for people of St Martin's parish. They are administered by the Burghley Estate and tenants live rent free. The L-shaped range of houses incorporates a chapel. These almshouses are on the site of the twelfth century hospital of St John the Baptist and St Thomas the Martyr, remains of which exist beneath the NE corner of the building. The west range of the houses was added in 1616. The rooms were rearranged and modernised in 1964/5. The building is of coursed rubble; six tall eighteenth century chimney stacks replace earlier stacks. Some windows are modern replacements; some are stone mullioned. On a jamb on a ground-floor window is a plaque reading: *Easter flood in the year 1640 the water came up to this mark.* (S)

Stamford: Lord Burghley's Bede Houses in Station Road were founded in 1597 for twelve poor old men and (unusually) their wives. The L shaped range of houses incorporates a chapel.

103.Stamford: f) **Williamson's Hospital**, St Peter's Street, founded 1770 by George Williamson for six poor widows *'as shall be as near to the age of 48 as shall be'.* This charity was established in the lifetime of Williamson (who died in 1768) as he permitted, when living, *'certain poor persons to reside rent free in a certain house leading to St Peter's Gate'.* It was described, in 1856, as an old irregular building. In 1787 James Hurst added to the bequest. It has now been sold and is no longer an almshouse. The building, which is early seventeenth century, is older than the foundation. A plaque reads: *Williams's Callis. These tenements were*

Stamford: Williamson's Callis was founded in 1770 in an early seventeenth century building. It is notable for a remarkable plaster ceiling in one of the rooms depicting a range of human figures, animals and fruit.

The group of three figures (top) is thought to be Susanna and the Elders. (Photos: D Peall) *adapted in 1762 by George Williamson grocer of this town, to house six poor widows.* It is a one storey building with semi-attics. The Stamford Mercury (May 1968) described it as 'an insignificant but historic Callis of no importance except for its fine ornate ceiling'. This Pevsner described as, 'robustly crude plasterwork with animals, fruit, and also Susanna and the Elders'. The 1851 Census gives the name of seven widows ranging in age from 65 to 79 who lived here; three were described 'late school mistress' or 'governess'; one had been a monthly nurse; another a charwoman[10]. (P)

104.Stickney: near Boston. Founded 1600 as **Steeping Charity** now **Stickney Consolidated Charities** which includes other small local charities which were amalgamated in 1966. William Steeping left a house and land for the poor and part of the land was exchanged at enclosure for land in the West Fen. The rent from land lying in Thorne Dale was originally distributed to the poor on 21st January and 25th March annually. The small charities included £29 left by the Revd John Robinson in 1811 for four poor women. A block of four bungalows was built in 1883 and there are also two pairs of semi-detached bungalows and a single bungalow built circa 1900. These almshouses are primarily for Stickney people but are now sometimes allotted to outsiders, also younger single men and women. (S)

105.Stoke Rochford: 6 miles south of Grantham. Almshouses founded by **Sir Edmund Turnor** in 1677 for six poor people each of whom received 1/- weekly and coals in 1905. Rebuilt in 1850/1. The 1881 Census Returns give Mary Mugridge, aged 52, as a resident. She was deaf from birth and was a dressmaker. (S)

106.Sutterton: (near Boston) **Sutterton Charity Trusts**: a) There was a row of cottages just off the main road overlooking the pools. These cottages dated from 1592 and were used partly as a workhouse, two cottages being kept for two poor widows who lived rent free. In 1938 the Trustees received a government grant of £682 and a loan of £341 from Boston Building Society for the restoration of this property. In 1956 there were seven cottages each consisting of a living room/kitchen, scullery and bedroom. Outside there was a washhouse and bucket closet. Lighting was then by oil lamp. The seven poor widows paid £2.2.6d per annum at that time but received £1 each at Christmas. The last resident died *c.* 1975 and the cottages were demolished. The money received for the site was taken into the Parochial Charities Fund which is used to give assistance to people in need. (X)

107.Sutterton: Sutterton Charity Trusts: b) In 1567 a William Whittingham and Giles Bogg purchased two cottages and gardens at Claydam on the understanding that they should be kept for the use of two poor widows who should pay 5/- per annum. In 1800 one of these cottages was pulled down and a blacksmith's shop, shed and yard was erected in its place. In 1956, one of the cottages and the blacksmith's shop were still there, on the right hand side of the road going into Sutterton, opposite the Cross Keys. At that date the blacksmith lived in the cottage at a rent of £14 per annum. Nothing now exists of **Bogg's cottages** and any income from the site was taken into the Parochial Charities Fund. (X)

108.Tallington: 4 miles northeast of Stamford. **Heron's Charity**, founded in 1582. Originally there were six ancient buildings; two were demolished to make way for three modern one-bedroom bungalows in 1970. The other four were sold for conversion by private owners. The bungalows are for the use of poor people who are resident in the parish of Tallington. (S)

109.Welby: near Grantham. Four almshouses were established by **William Welby** in 1780 for four poor widows at the west end of the Main Street. From 1869 a school was part of the charity. In the 1871 census one of the residents was Martha Storer and her four children. The houses were demolished in July 1966 and some of the stonework was incorporated in a bus shelter opposite the site in 1968. (X)

110.Whaplode: The parish register for 1624 records: *This year almshouses were built with money left by William Tashe gent.* In 1837 they were said to be much in need of repair. In 1856 White's Directory records that the houses were for six poor women and Sir Anthony Irby had charged his estates with their reparation. In 1872, 10d each was paid to two almswomen. One of them, Ann Atkinson, died that year in her 103rd year. The 1881 Census gives Sarah Wright aged 82 as a resident in Mill Gate Almshouse. Kelly's 1905 directory states there are almshouses for six poor widows built by an ancestor of

Whaplode: This row of six almshouses in Churchgate, originally built in 1624, was repaired many times over the centuries. It was demolished and replaced by modern bungalows in the mid twentieth century.
(Photo: Mrs Nellie Hoyes)

Lord Boston two of whom received 10d a week from a charity left by Sir Anthony Irby. The charity now incorporates the Elias Wilson Charity (1704) and Whaplode Parochial Charities. The present bungalows were built on the site of a row of six houses in Churchgate and are intended for the widows of agricultural workers. (S)

Wragby: Edmund Turnor founded an almshouse in Wragby in 1697 for six clergy widows and six lay widows or widowers of Wragby. It was rebuilt in Gothic style in 1840.

111. Worlaby: near Brigg. A hospital was founded by **John Lord Belasye** Baron of Worlaby in 1663 for four poor women. Each inmate received 2/- weekly in 1905. The property, in 1905, belonged to the Duke of Newcastle. In Kelly's 1933 directory it was stated that the house was, *'under the control and direction of the vicar and two trustees; each inmate receives 2/- per week: the property is now vested in the church'.* The almshouses fell out of use and, by the early 1960s, the buildings had become semi-derelict. An order was served on the Trustees by Glanford Brigg RDC in 1966 as the building was unfit for human habitation. The building is listed grade I and could not be demolished, but it was considered to be too expensive for the Trustees to restore. After taking advice it was decided to sell the buildings and a parcel of land for a nominal sum. In 1969 a buyer was found and the Trustees received a cheque for £446.15.3d. The almshouse is now a private house. In 1981 the charity known as the hospital of John, Lord Belasye founded 1663, was merged with the charity of William Cook and the combined charity became known as the Belasyse-Cook Charity. Few claims were made in the following year as the distribution of income was limited to needy women in the parish of Worlaby, therefore, a change was made in the provision under the Objects of the Charity clause and the funds are now in a healthy state and available to people from neighbouring villages. For instance payments have been made for travelling expenses to parents of sick children. The original need is no longer apparent but a sensible modernisation of the fund has given the Trustees more scope in the present day. (P)

112.Wragby: 11 miles east of Lincoln. In 1697 **Sir Edmund Turnor** founded a chapel and almshouses for six clergy widows and six lay widows or widowers of Wragby. In 1708 an endowment was made. The houses were rebuilt in 1840 in Gothic style at a cost of £1,950 out of funds accumulated from unappropriated pensions. In 1905, 25/- per quarter was paid to clergy widows and 16/8d per quarter to lay widows. The latter also received £5 per annum bequeathed by the wife of a former vicar, Mrs Yard. £40 per annum was also paid to the vicar to be Chaplain to the houses. One of the rules for the inmates reads: *That each of them do strictly abstain from ale and strong drink and take no more thereof than what is needful for their health and the support and comfort of their spirits.* The houses were modernised in 1988 and continue to function. There is no longer a warden. A mortgage for modernisation was obtained from The Housing Corporation but this has been transferred to a building society. Tenants pay a modest rent. [The Turnors continued a tradition of benevolence to the poor. Christopher Turnor esq. (died 1886) had a library and reading room built in 1856 for the benefit of working men and others]. (S)

Wrangle: These almshouses at Joy Hill were built as four single dwellings but have since been converted to form two dwellings. There are also two twentieth century bungalows on Joy Hill, built as almshouses.

113.Wrangle: Alenson's Charity. Thomas Alenson's will dated 1555 created a Trust which was supplemented by a bequest of nine acres in 1705 from the Revd W Erskine. Does anything exist now? Three men and two women received 6d and 5d each weekly and 5/- at Christmas in lieu of a gown. Up to 1833 cows were provided and pastured on a piece of land called Little Pingall. In 1837 the almshouse was said to be in a dilapidated state. It contained four apartments; a fifth member of the community was the schoolmaster who had a house erected for his accommodation. There are, in 2002, four almshouses in good condition; two of these are converted from the original four single-storey brick cottages and there are also two post-war brick bungalows. All four dwellings are at Joy Hill. Residents must be of good character and of the parishes of Wrangle, Old Leake or New Leake. (S)

114.Wyberton: Wyberton near Boston. **William Field's**: four cottages were rebuilt in 1871 in Church Lane from a bequest by William Field in 1624 for four poor widows each of whom received 3/6d in 1905. Now rebuilt in co-operation with the Borough Council who gave land at a nominal fee. Known as United Charities incorporating Field/Anderson/Tooley. (S)

Wyberton: Four almshouses founded by William Field in 1624 were rebuilt in 1871 (top). This building (now converted to form a privately owned single dwelling) was replaced by modern bungalows (lower) administered by United Charities in 1972.

1800 - 2000 :
From Picturesque To Plain

The 'Orme' Bedehouses in Louth stand on the site of the town's prison at the junction of Eastgate and Ramsgate. They were founded by the Revd Frederick Orme in 1885 and designed by James Fowler in Jacobean style.

During the nineteenth century many attractive almshouses were founded or rebuilt including Belton (1839); Dawson's almshouses at Grantham (1862); Heckington (1888) and many more. Architecturally the general aim in the nineteenth century was to provide attractive housing. Some groups were designed by eminent architects such as St Anne's Bedehouses in Lincoln (1847), designed by A W N Pugin. The Orme Almshouses in Louth were designed by James Fowler - one of the foremost Victorian architects in the county. In Belton the almshouses were built in estate style ... Barchester arrived in Lincolnshire. The tradition of almshouse building continued into the twentieth century in spite of the increasingly widespread provision of council housing. Almshouse trustees take their duties seriously and their residents thoroughly enjoy the benefits including pleasant and historic surroundings.

Workhouses and Houses of Industry were a large-scale way of housing the impotent poor, mainly in the eighteenth and nineteenth centuries. They are not covered in this book. Similarly, houses provided by the parish, known as Poor Houses, are not included. It is presumed that, in Lincolnshire, such houses would generally be of mud and stud construction and none are known to survive.

There is another small group of houses that fall between two categories. These are houses that were originally almshouses but whose responsibility was taken over by the overseers of the poor; Sturton by Stow and Haxey are in this group. Another example impossible to categorise and not included in this list are the old cottages (now demolished) at Willingham by Stow which were known as almshouses into the twentieth century but were maintained by the parish. However, no record can be found of any charitable trust relating to them, and there are probably many more like this. An example of housing for the poor which links parish care, through the Vestry, with private charity, is that of Alkborough. That link, with its original intent to make a small provision for the dispossessed, continues today although modern recipients are not in quite the needy category of their predecessors. Winteringham too had a row of six cottages known as The Almshouses although there is no documentation to show their origins. They

These cottages at Willingham by Stow (now demolished) were known as almshouses into the twentieth century, but there is no record of any charitable trust relating to them. There must be many cases of such 'unofficial' almshouses (usually maintained by the parish) in Lincolnshire villages. (Photo: Kathleen Taylor)

consisted of a single room with space in the roof; there was a well in front of them and three chimney stacks. From 1900 until their demolition c 1960, when they were replaced by four council bungalows, they were administered by the Parish Council. They must have been built by the Scarbrough family, probably after enclosure in 1761.

Almshouses and bedehouses were generally well-built and high status structures dedicated to their founder. By the nineteenth century they were also intended as picturesque additions to the landscape. The Orme almshouses in Louth, for instance, designed by James Fowler, are set in an acre of ornamental gardens.

The almshouses at Aylesby, built in 1925, are in eighteenth century vernacular style with a fine Doric colonnade. (Photo: Roy Jackson)

Many older foundations were rebuilt in the nineteenth and early twentieth centuries. Alford, founded in 1668, was rebuilt in 1870; Aylesby was a very late foundation in 1925 but was built in eighteenth century style with a Doric colonnade; Kingerby founded in 1675 was rebuilt in the twentieth century. There are many more examples. Of particular note was a spurt of rebuilding in the 1820s, 1830s and 1840s in Stamford and Spalding. Three of note in Stamford are: Truesdale's which was founded in 1700 but rebuilt in 1833; Burghley's, founded in 1597 had a range rebuilt in the northeastern corner (architect Edward Browning) in 1849; and Snowden's, founded in 1604, was rebuilt in 1822. These three examples were all rebuilt in local stone. They are solidly made with good quality materials, and simply and pleasantly ornamented - they are pleasing to the eye and assets to the town. Specifications for the rebuilding of Gamlyn's almshouse in Church Street, Spalding in 1844 include the following details: *best red stock bricks in Flemish bond towards the street, proper drains; foundations on firm and solid ground; damp-proof course in slate laid in Roman cement; jambs, door heads, sills and mullions, angled pinnacles and gable coping to be of tooled ashlar; entrance lobbies to be laid with 3" tooled Yorkshire flags; small fireplace to be made in the corner of each scullery – all work to be completed in a good and substantial workmanlike manner with best materials of their several kinds.* The builders were William Sharman, John Sharp and Stephen Dawson; the architect Joseph Mitchell of Sheffield (fee £100). There was, however, a sequel to this rebuilding as the architect was recalled after complaints of smoking chimneys. He decided that the builders had, literally, cut corners and the chimneys were rebuilt.

The tradition of good quality work generally continues and most almshouses are of good, modern standard. The conversion of houses in Church Street, Spalding, into flats in 1939 showed the beginning of a trend to rearrange accommodation to different requirements. Formerly males were housed in houses to the east; women to the west and couples in the centre. Now the sexes are housed according to need and availability not dependent on gender. The 1939 specification was encouraging; work was to be completed: *in a thorough workmanlike manner, all works with materials specified otherwise with the best materials.*

Architecture changes and perhaps it is unfair to compare box-bungalows built in the latter half of the twentieth century with the picturesque buildings of a previous era but it must be said that the extra attention given then, to mullions, gables and general appearance, bestows more pleasure on the eye.

Urban almshouses of the late nineteenth century often adopted a vernacular style. The Fishermen's

This neat terrace in Grimsby is an urban almshouse – built in 1896, the 'Fishermen's Houses' are still thought of as desirable by local people and there is a waiting list for occupation.

In the late nineteenth and early twentieth centuries, the neo-gothic style was often favoured by almshouse builders, as here at the Godson Almshouses on Heckington village green.

Houses in Grimsby, well-built and unpretentious terraced rows, are still regarded as desirable by local people.

The style of buildings seemed to change abruptly after the First World War. The Godson almshouses in Heckington erected in 1886 and 1904 respectively are in Victorian Gothic or cottage ornée style as are most others of that date such as the Teetotal houses in Ruskington, 1887, and the Scott houses in the same village, 1904. In nearby Billingborough, however, the Woolley accommodation erected in 1919 just after the war are plain brick maisonettes built straight onto the pavement – well-built but in utilitarian style. Similarly the Frow houses in Gainsborough, 1925, are built on a small plot straight onto the street. The pattern of no-frills building continues through the twentieth century with modern bungalows, where the emphasis is more on convenience than appearance – see Wyberton and Fosdyke. Where once a productive garden might have been considered an asset, it is now acknowledged that older people generally prefer double-glazing and central heating to land which they are often unable to cultivate.

It has been suggested, by an elderly farmer, that many early and middle twentieth century almshouse endowments, made as provision primarily for farm workers, were to fill the gap left by disbanding the workhouses. He could remember widows going into the workhouse when their husbands died as the tied cottages in which they had lived, were needed for the new workers. Now that there are fewer workers on the land, and many farm workers own their own houses or have council houses, this need has largely disappeared.

Where houses have a scanty endowment many Trusts have converted into Housing Associations and obtained grants for modernising premises. Some, such as the Anderson Almshouses at Lea returned literally to the earth as the cost of maintenance could not be met. Others were sold privately and ceased to be almshouses, such as Worlaby and the Catholic Almshouses at Market Rasen.

Catholic almshouses at Market Rasen founded by David Young in 1845. It is now a private house called 'Young's Cottage' in memory of the founder.

The maintenance contribution required by most, but not all, almshouse trusts means that almshouse residents are not tenants on lease but licence holders. In theory this means that a resident can be ejected but, in practice, few trustees can recall this having been necessary in living memory.

Wardens are now few and far between; Browne's (Stamford), St Anne's (Lincoln) and Lord Burghley's (Stamford) are among the handful that still maintain the tradition. Perhaps it is not coincidence that these three groups also still maintain a chapel. Now, most residents are telephone users and some are equipped with a 'Lifeline' system whereby they can call for help if they fall ill or are in distress. Some local councils are now considering reinstating peripatetic wardens for their elderly tenants and this system will incorporate almshouse residents.

Indoor lavatories are now standard but provision in the past would have probably have been a shared privy at best! One nineteenth century specification mentions a *'double necessary house*

Some almshouses were founded specifically for women. Miss Mary Anne Scotney founded these almshouses at Market Deeping in 1876 for six Protestant women, being either unmarried or widows. The residents are still single or widowed women.

of boards with a brick vault'. In another there is a reference to a *'little house'*.

For whom were the almshouses intended? Foundations vary somewhat in their criteria but generally the inmates were to be poor and old in order to qualify. Houses founded by women were usually for the use of women e.g. Belton; Bradley's

Frow's Almshouses in Gainsborough are unique in the county in being founded specifically for members of the Congregational Church.

almshouses in Grantham; Hemingby and Market Deeping. Male founders often favoured women too *e.g.* St Anne's bedehouses in Lincoln, founded by Revd Richard Waldo Sibthorp in memory of his mother, was for fourteen females of limited means and Wragby founded by Sir Edmund Turnor was for widows. A few founders specified men *e.g.* St Poll hospital at Market Rasen was for eight indigent men and in Louth the almshouses were for ten poor men. Sometimes religion is specified - perhaps Protestantism can be assumed but there was provision made for Catholic inmates at Market Rasen and Irnham. Bradley's almshouses in Grantham were for Anglican females. Gainsborough (Frow's Almshouses) was unique in that provision was made for members of the Congregational church. Some provided housing for males and females and one, Tattershall, mentions families. Boston has one of the few almshouses for a group selected by occupation *i.e.* The Muster Roll Houses for aged seamen and widows as is the large foundation in Grimsby. One of these houses is one of only three groups in the

Owston Almshouse was founded by Miss Frances Sanders in 1860 for six aged females of good character. They were expected to attend church and help with fruit picking. A ridge tile on the almshouse shows one such good woman, dutifully reading her bible! (Photo: D. Peall)

county which was raised by Methodist donations and all are in the same coastal area. The cottage homes at Cleethorpes had strong Methodist connections and the Flottergate Benevolent Homes (Haycroft Street) Grimsby were a Methodist foundation in 1933.

In return for their gifts most benefactors hoped for gratitude and decency but the aged beneficiaries of Bank's Almshouses at Revesby were also required to help with the hay harvest if fit enough to do so. There is no record of this obligation being enforced. In Owston Ferry the residents of the Sanders' almshouses funded in 1860, were expected to help with fruit picking at the founder's family home.

An interesting insight into the social status of bedeswomen is provided by a letter dated 1870, sent to the Revd J Fowler by R W Sibthorp (founder of the St Anne's Bedehouse in Lincoln). *'I shall miss Mrs D when I next call at the Bede-houses, for we had always a cheerful chat together, joking about a pigeon pie... I am not certain whether I shall attend the next meeting ... I see no objection whatever, but the contrary, to the bringing in of decayed gentlewomen; but each Trustee, whose turn it may be to appoint, can and might be advised by any one interested in St Anne's utility as an almshouse to look out for such. I should like myself to see this rather higher grade, if such can be found within the limits of locality fixed by the trust deeds. But I doubt if this would be, e.g. in the case of Canwick or Harmston and Waddington. And some, indeed much, consideration must be give to the admixture of two classes, which would cause annoyances to both. If, as I now sometimes wish, these Bede-houses had been 'open to all England,' to use a common phrase; proper objects in decayed gentlewomen, would have presented themselves by the dozen. Even baronets' widows are now seeking the pittance of £20 or £25 a year given by a charity in London; and such must feel the privations of penury. A baronet's daughter, of one of the oldest Lincolnshire families, who had been presented at the Court of George II, died an almswoman at Brigg in my remembrance.'* The inference is that decayed gentlewomen would not be found in the villages but they might be found countrywide. As far as I can ascertain the baronet's widow was unique in her class in the county in becoming a bedeswoman but it is difficult to find evidence of social class amongst others. In the absence of other evidence it might reasonably be assumed that the majority of bedespeople were of humble origins.

St Anne's Bedehouses in Lincoln were founded in 1847 by Revd Richard Waldo Sibthorp and built to a design by A. W. N. Pugin. The founder was keen to encourage a 'better' class of residents – or 'decayed gentlewomen' as he put it! (Photo: D. Peall)

In the twentieth and twenty-first centuries needs have changed and almshouse trustees have noted the change and are sensitive to it. The ancient, beautiful Middlecot's Hospital on the banks of the Witham at Fosdyke for example, although an attractive building, is in rather a remote position for old people of today, so the replacement bungalows are now sited in the centre of the villages of Fosdyke and Algarkirk. The original almshouse has been sold and converted into three pleasant apartments for car-owning residents. Several trustees reported that it was not always easy nowadays to fulfil both age and residency qualifications as people of pensionable age tended to be already provided for. So the rules may occasionally be bent a little or changed to suit modern needs. At Alford, for instance, it has been mooted that younger people in need, perhaps single parents, might now qualify for the housing on offer. Again the Grimsby Fishermen's Houses are an exception to the rule. Cook's directory of 1902 states that in one block of houses six widows lived with forty one children and, in another block, seven widows with thirty children. These days the position in Grimsby is reversed, in keeping with

It is often said that almshouses tend to promote longevity. Mrs Nellie Simpson, a resident of St Anne's Bedehouses in Lincoln, still walked weekly to the Post Office to collect her pension at the grand age of 101. (Photo: D. Peall)

the demographic changes, and most residents are now elderly.

Almshouses, on what evidence is available, appear to promote longevity. The ages of pensioners in the Orme Almshouse in Louth included many men in their 80s and Ann Atkinson died in her almshouse in Whaplode in 1872 in her 103rd year. In a history of Tattershall, 1891, by a Mrs Pickworth, the longevity of the inhabitants of the Bedehouses there is remarked upon. In the preceding thirty years their ages were said to range from 90 to 97. A current example (2001) is of Mrs Nellie Simpson a resident in St Anne's Bedehouses, Lincoln, who, at the age of 101 walked weekly to the Post Office to collect her pension and regularly visited her friend Daisy May, 104, who at the end of her life, moved to a nursing home after a long residence at St Anne's. Nellie has enjoyed the peace and security of St Anne's for 33 years to date. The gravestones in the grounds of St Anne's give further testimony to the longevity of its residents.

Almshouses are now seen as picturesque additions to the landscape, an alternative to a Housing Association bungalow. Some are privately owned and consist of several cottages knocked into one house *e.g.* four almshouses at Cockerington are now one house; the ten houses that were once the Middlecott Hospital at Fosdyke are now three private houses. Most almshouses seem to be prized by tenants and neighbours in town or village enjoy the sight of well-built cottages. The founders' objectives appear to be satisfied; their names have survived and deserving tenants are still decently housed.

Almshouses are successful survivors. The formula must have contained the right elements. The showcase social housing of past centuries no longer requires a uniform to be worn, church attendance is not compulsory, doles are now a matter for the state, bathrooms have been installed ... but people still like the idea of almshouses.

In June 1986 a service of thanksgiving was held in Westminster Abbey in the presence of Her Majesty, Queen Elizabeth, the Queen Mother, to celebrate 1000 years of almshouse provision in England.

Most charities are now ruled by 'the scheme' which is a formal statement of the charity's purpose and gives its trustees, their duties and responsibilities, and the trust's assets and income.

Modern trustees of almshouses strive to provide good housing for deserving people. Time and again I heard from trustees of the help received from The Almshouse Association, a non-statutory advisory body formed in 1946 for mutual assistance following the ravages of wartime bombing. The aims of the Association are;

- to preserve the historic tradition of almshouses
- to promote the welfare and independence of residents
- to provide good quality housing for needy people
- to manage charitable resources as effectively as possible

It must be largely, or partly, due to this organisation that almshouses are still thriving today.

In all the gazetteers, the status of the building is indicated by a letter, thus:

X *Building no longer exists*

S *Still in use as an almshouse (but may be a rebuilding of original)*

P *Building survives but not now in use as an almshouse*

GAZETTEER

Almshouses founded 1800-2000

115.Alkborough on the east side of the Trent 18 miles northwest of Brigg: In 1768 Alkborough was enclosed by Act of Parliament and there was a small loss of grazing for poor cottagers as a result. In the Enclosure Agreement it was written that these cottagers should receive a small annual sum (£1.12s) in lieu of grazing rights, the cost to be met by the owners of Walcot, a small hamlet containing the seat of a gentleman Thomas Goulton. This charge was transferred to the owners of Alkborough Manor Farm in the 1920s and, in 1977, when the farm was sold, a charge of £40 was levied and invested by the Charity Commissioners in the Parish Estate. This amount was then combined with the remnants of Lady Strickland's almshouse charity. In 1837 the bedehouses were described as an old house divided into ten tenements with one rood of garden, occupied by parish paupers. In 1846 according to a survey by a John Nutchey there were two groups of houses for the poor in the village. One group was known as bedehouses (six cottages), the other group (five cottages) were administered by the Overseers of the Poor. In 1862 the Vestry voted to give their rights to almshouses to Lady Strickland (great niece of Thomas Goulton of Walcot) provided she was willing to build six more almshouses for widows - residents to be chosen jointly by Lady Strickland and the parish. Apparently the Town Houses (administered by the Overseers) were demolished in 1864 and a

Alkborough: These cottages opposite the Church are thought to be the almshouses founded by Lady Strickland in 1862. The charity still exists but the cottages are no longer almshouses.

notice was nailed to the church door to this effect. The site of these houses still belongs to the parish and is now converted into an amenity area for the village. Other houses, according to the Town's Book of Accounts, were sold in 1865, the year in which Lady Strickland died. As a result £221. 5s.11d. was invested in 3% Consols. Oral tradition suggests that three cottages opposite the church gate built of stone and pantiles by the Walcot estate were the cottages built to honour Lady Strickland's agreement. It is not known when they ceased to be almshouses but the charity, combined with the enclosure money and Consols, is still administered intermittently in the form of packets of tea. The last distribution was to pensioners for a millennium gift in 2000. (P)

116.Aylesby near Grimsby: **Francis Willmer McAulay Memorial Cottages**. 1925. Seven cottages in eighteenth century vernacular

Aylesby: Seven cottages were built in 18th century vernacular style in memory of Captain Francis Willmer McAulay who was killed in action in the First World War.

style with a colonnade of Doric columns at the back and spacious grounds including a orchard. Intended for the use of farm-workers but in 2001 only one ex-farm-worker is resident – other residents are of various occupations. Administered by the

Grimsby Fishermen's Dependent Fund. An inscription on the front of the building reads: *In memory of Francis Willmer McAulay Captain RFA TF who fell in action at Fonquevillers France on May 21st 1916 aged 25.* (S)

117.Barnoldby le Beck: Leslie K Osmond Memorial Bungalows. Two bungalows in the centre of the village, which is a commuter village serving Grimsby. The inscription on the side of one bungalow reads: *These bungalows were bequeathed to the village by Alderman Leslie K Osmond of Barnoldby le Beck erected 1968.* (S)

118.Billingborough – 9 miles equidistant between Bourne and Sleaford: Mary Jane Woolley under a will of 1914 had almshouses erected in memory of her parents. These were for twelve poor persons; six lone women were to live in the 'Low Nests' and six lone men in the 'High Nests'. The persons were to be of excellent character, capable of helping themselves and preferably members of the Church of England. The governors were to be three ladies and the vicar and churchwardens of the parish. Interest of £400 Consols (Consolidated Stock: Government securities raised from various taxes), in the hands of the Charity Commissioners, was to provide for the upkeep and repair of the premises. These conditions were written on a stone tablet placed in the church. The accommodation is now improved and made into maisonettes for the Billingborough parishioners. It was commended by the Charity Commissioners in 2000 for the excellence of the improvements. (S)

Billingborough: Founded in 1914, six lone women to were to live in the 'Low Nests' with six lone men in the 'High Nests'. The building is still an almshouse and was commended in 2000 for the excellence of its recent conversion.

119.Boston: a) **Muster Roll Houses** off Skirbeck Road were for nine aged seamen and widows who lived rent-free. They were built in 1846. All seamen belonging to the port contributed monthly to the Merchant Seamen's Fund. When a cottage became vacant they were allocated to those men, or their widows, who had contributed longest to the fund. In 1990 these houses were demolished to a headline 'Joy over demolition' in the Boston Citizen. Planning permission was obtained for the construction of new almshouses by an organisation called The Order of Malta Homes Trust comprising eight flats and ten bungalows. The Order of Malta Trust has now (2001) asked the Leonard Hackett Memorial Trust to take over trusteeship. The latter Trust was established to 'rescue' Almshouse Charities in difficulties. When the trusteeship is completed it is hoped that up to eight new almshouses will be built on the site. (S)

Boston: Horton's Almshouse comprised twelve, one bed-roomed bungalows, founded in 1893 by Miss Harriet Horton. (Photo: Alberta MacKillie)

120.Boston: b)**Horton's Almshouse Charity**, Frieston Road – 12 one-bedroom bungalows built 1908; founded by Miss Harriet Horton

Boston: The Willoughby Road Almshouses, along the Maud Foster Drain, replaced the tenements which previously comprised St Leonard's Hospital in the 1860s and 1870s. *(Photo: Alberta MacKillie)*

in 1893. Single women or married couples over 60 are eligible to live here. In 1956 residents lived rent free and received 30/- at Christmas. At that date the houses were still lit by gas. (S)

121.Boston: c) **Willoughby Road Almshouses:** These are the successors to St Leonard's Hospital, Hospital Bridge. The old tenements were pulled down and rebuilt by Mr and Mrs B S Simpson [Mr Simpson was a local solicitor] and Mr J R Rawson [a local bank director] at a cost of £950 in the 1860s and 70s. There are two semi-detached pairs of cottages, with date-stones *J R R 1873* and *B S S 1869*, also a row of six *In Memoriam 1874*. In 1876 each bedesmen received 1/6d per week from the endowment. There were ten bedesmen and, in some cases, their wives. In 1913 there were ten small tenements with gardens attached, situated on Maud Foster Drainside. The payment at this date appears to have decreased to 1/- per week. The almshouses are still in use. They consist of a group of four with a separate pair at either end in red brick with polychromatic yellow brick and tile bands. They have Welsh slate roofs and the windows have yellow brick reveals with painted stone sills and flush chamfered lintels. (S)

122.Brant Broughton: 12 miles equidistant between Sleaford and Lincoln – In 1860 Sir John Sutton had six almshouses built for poor widows, the houses to be let at 2/- per year. The houses are modernised and updated as funds allow. There is no land endowment. Preference is given to elderly people with family connections in the village but currently (2001) there are insufficient elderly, single, applicants so three of the houses are let to younger people who sign a contract agreeing to vacate the premises if an older person applies. The trustees will provide new domestic equipment when necessary. (S)

123.Cleethorpes: a) **The Cottage Homes**, Coronation Road – built to commemorate the coronation of Edward VII in 1902 largely as a result of Methodist initiative. Some houses were given by individual donors and some by public subscription. The original trustees were all donors and in 2001 some of the trustees are descendants of the original committee. The new trust deeds of 1946 invited representatives of the original donors to become trustees and several accepted. There are twelve houses, still almshouses. They originally had slate roofs but have now been re-roofed in pantiles. They are intended for the use of people from Cleethorpes and many applications are received although rarely nowadays from fishermen for whom the houses were first built. In 1979 Major Henry Leonard Holloway left a legacy towards these houses in memory of his wife. Other legacies have been received and in the early 1970s considerable modernisation was undertaken. At this time the residents volunteered to pay a small maintenance contribution and this small voluntary amount has stayed at the same level for thirty years. The houses always had a Methodist as Honorary Secretary of the Trustees, the first one being Mr Ernest Benjamin Chapman. (S)

124.**Cleethorpes**: b) **Coronation Houses**, Mill Road – Eight houses were built to commemorate the coronation of George V in 1911. These houses are administered by the trustees of the Coronation Road Cottage Homes and the same information is relevant. (S)

125.**Colsterworth:** Almshouses for four widows were erected in 1861 by Christopher Turnor of Panton Hall. There is a row of four stone cottages set back from the main road, with a central date-stone. At some time in the 1950s/60s the foundation documents were examined and it was concluded that there was no obligation to continue with these houses as almshouses. Consequently they do not have charitable status and are now commercially let to applicants to the Stoke Rochford Estate. (P)

126.**Deeping St James**: 6 miles from Stamford: **Providence Homes**, Broadgate – six brick bungalows in a terrace built 1956 from a gift by Miss H E Smith in memory of the late Mr M D Smith and family of Deeping St James for the benefit of Deeping St James' people. Residents must have lived in Deeping St James or the surrounding villages for at least two years; they can be single, or a couple, over the age of 55. (S)

127.**Donington on Bain**: 7 miles southwest of Louth: **Harold True Almshouse Charity** founded 1981, bungalow built 1982. Harold True was born in Donington in 1889; he served in the First World War, married but was childless. On his death in 1965 he left his estate to his wife on trust and on her death the estate was for the benefit of the aged, poor and infirm of the parish of Donington-on-Bain. The two-bedroom brick bungalow was built by local builders Goodwin and Tucker. (S)

128.**Epworth**: Pinfold Street (now an extension of Rectory Street). The 1881 census returns give Sarah Wilmot, 74, a labourer's widow as resident in the almshouses. By 1891 (Census) there is no reference to almshouses here. The cottages were apparently owned by a Mr Wilson in the twentieth century and were sold and demolished in the 1960s. (X)

129.**Fishtoft:** near Boston: Four charity cottages were rebuilt in 1828 at a cost of £110. They were occupied rent-free, in 1856, by poor parishioners. They stood near the 'Red Cow' at the end of Old School Lane. In 1956 they were said to be in very bad repair. Two of the cottages consisted of one room up and one down with a sink in the downstairs room. The other two cottages had two rooms up and two down. They had electric light and outside lavatories. They were pulled down and not replaced sometime in the latter part of the twentieth century. (X)

130.**Fishtoft:** near Boston: two dwellings known as **Coronation Cottages** were built in 1911 for about £300. They are an adjoining pair of three bedroomed houses, built of brick with slate roofs. The cost of maintaining these houses was taking too much of the Charity's income so they were sold with the approval of the Charity Commissioners and the money raised was invested with the Charity Official Investment Fund. The houses were sold in 1990 and 1993 respectively. (P)

131.**Fotherby**: 3 miles north of Louth: **Allenby Almshouses** erected in 1866 for six poor people on the site of the former vicarage. Each occupant was to receive 9/- per week. Applications had to be over 60 and live, or have lived in the village. Married couples or spinsters were acceptable but single men were not. The founder, Everitt Allenby, was a wealthy businessman who lived in Surrey but was a native of Fotherby. His brother, John, also left an endowment for beef, flour and coals for the residents. The almshouses still function as such. (P)

132.**Friskney:** 4 miles southwest of Wainfleet: United Charities incorporating: a) **Eliza Gardiner's Almshouses, b) Mantle Green c) Poor Land Almshouses; d) John Shaw's Almshouses**. In all there are 21 almshouses in the village (Eliza Gardiner's from a bequest in 1935 were rebuilt in the 1950s; twelve in Mantle Green built in three phases in the 1990s). The Mantle Green bungalows were financed by capital released by the sale of land by the trustees of the Poors' Land Trust; there was an additional bungalow here bequeathed by V C Farrow. The accommodation is in single and double units. (S)

133.Gainsborough:– **Frow Charity**. Money was left by M A Frow, corn merchant, for the erection of three houses on land adjoining the John Robinson Memorial Church (Congregational) in Gladstone Street. The houses were opened with a dedication service in February 1926. The plaque on the central porch reads: *To the Glory of God and in memory of George and Mary Frow* (Miss Frow's parents). The newspaper report carried a specification of the buildings which were to be 'a domestic adjunct to the Memorial Church and school. Externally the building has been arranged not to be out of harmony with the present buildings, but a little more domestic in appearance, and perhaps a little more English in character.' Moulded bricks were used to the doors and windows with Ancaster moulded stone sills. The roof had Cornish green slates and 'boldly over-hanging eaves to the front'. The latest technology was employed with the back roofs of concrete reinforced with expanded metal and covered with Val de Travers Asphalt. Each house had a living room, bedroom, entrance passage and bathroom plus scullery and larder. Gas rings and coppers were fitted and white glazed sinks. Local gentry, in the form of Sir Hickman Bacon, attended the opening ceremony and Mr J T Kettle (Chairman of the Lincolnshire Congregational Union) who conducted the service spoke of the uniqueness of the occasion and bequest. He spoke of the need for such houses being built for aged people. It was remarked that the houses were built near to the church 'so that their aged friends might be able to attend the Church they loved and at which they worshipped.' The site of the John Robinson Church was once the site of All Saints' vicarage which was sold by the Church Commissioners. Because of this the John Robinson Church and the almshouses are adjacent to parish church land making the position of the almshouses traditional – yet unique in their Congregational foundation. During 1981/2 the houses were updated for modern living and now comprise a bed-sitting room with kitchen and bathroom. They are all single units. The residence qualifications were changed in 1969 as there were insufficient members of the John Robinson congregation to fill the vacancies. Preference for applicants is now given to a) Members of the United Reformed Church of Gainsborough (once known as the Congregational Church) b) Members of the United Reformed Church in Lincolnshire c) Members of any church in Gainsborough. Present residents (AD 2000) include a Salvation Army member, a Methodist and a Roman Catholic. No age limit is specified but, in practice, all residents are over retirement age. Because the endowment was not large enough for maintenance the Trust formed a Housing Association in 1981 and this enabled them to obtain a grant for renovation from the Housing Corporation. Residents pay a maintenance contribution to assist in the costs of upkeep. (S)

134.Goxhill: (date unknown) – 5 miles from Barton on the bank of the Humber: At some date prior to 1837 there were four almshouses here which were maintained by **William Markham** in his lifetime. Inmates then received 2/6d and two bags of coal [how frequently is not known] but no bequest was left for the maintenance of this charity. The Charity Commissioners stated that a copy of Markham's will was obtained but it contained no bequest whatsoever to the poor of Goxhill or any other place. The almshouses were probably maintained by him during his life but he does not appear to have made any provision for their continuance. (X)

135.Grantham: a) **Bradley's Almshouses,** which were in High Street, were endowed by Elizabeth widow of Richard in 1874. Six females aged not less than 63, must be members of the Church of England and previous residents of Boston or Little Gonerby. Each inmate received £1 monthly (1905). Eight modern units were erected in Swinegate in 1964. An inscription over the door reads: *The houses were built by the Trustees of the Grantham Almshouses Charities and paid for by the sale of original almshouses in High Street which were founded by Elizabeth Bradley in 1874.* This complex became known as the **Dorothy Brownlow Almshouses** because Lord Brownlow had given the land in memory of his wife. (S)

Grantham: Dawson's Almshouses were erected in 1862 to house ten poor and aged persons. They were modernised in 1967 and the number of dwellings was reduced to eight.

136.Grantham: b) **Dawson's Almshouses**, Brook Street, erected in 1862 by trustees of Dawson Charity. Money was left by George Dawson in 1662 for ten poor and aged persons. The charity was revised in 1844 and again in 1860 when a new scheme was devised by the Charity Commissioners. In 1862 ten almshouses were built. The 1881 Census Return gives Letitia Winter, unmarried, 85, as a resident. The residents of each house received 6/- weekly in 1905. Income was derived from a farm at Gosberton. In 1967 the almshouses were modernised and the number was reduced to eight. (S)

137.Grimsby: a)**The Fishermen and Sailors' Harbour of Refuge,** Castle Street, The Square and Weelsby Street. These almshouses were for the benefit of fishermen's widows and orphans, also aged fishermen and their wives. The scheme was set up in 1896 and is unique in its foundation. The opening of ten houses was performed in 1897 (Queen Victoria's diamond jubilee year) by Mr Grant Thorold the donor of the land. In his opening speech Mr Thorold commented that until there was protection for the widow and her family the morals of the town would never be any better. It appears that sixteen houses were already in occupation at this time, the first being occupied in 1893, and 48 were planned in total. Money was raised by appeal and substantial donors had their names inscribed on the houses and their remarks recorded by the local paper, The Grimsby Evening Telegraph. One house was named John Wesley House on behalf of the Wesleyan Methodists of the town. The initiative came from The Fishermen and Sailors' Harbour of Refuge led by the Port Missionary, Mr J Davies, known locally as the Fishermen's Bishop. The terms of the deed stated that no applications were to be ineligible on account of religious belief. The Trust was always non-sectarian. The donors were many and included whole houses given by individuals and organisations such as the Dock Committee. The Earl of Yarborough was one donor in 1901 when the last six houses were occupied. The Ellis family, timber merchants, were also big donors. The houses in Weelsby Street and the cottages in Castle Street and The Square nearby are all lived in. They are kept in good repair and there is a waiting list for possession. Many of the residents, but not all, are still connected with the sea and the fishing trade. Cook's Directory of 1902 stated that thirteen widows with 71 children occupied the houses and 20 aged couples were in the bungalows. The charity is now run by The Grimsby and District Homes for the Poor

Grimsby: The Aged Fishermen's Houses in The Square. The scheme to protect fishermen's widows and orphans and also aged fishermen and their wives was unique when it was set up in 1896. Many of the current residents are still connected with the sea or fishing.

and Aged Workers in the Fish Trade who also run the Diamond Jubilee Provident Homes in Doughty Road. In all 43 living units are provided. This includes the addition of six flats in Weelsby Court which were added to the trust c. 1995 as funds were available. A maintenance contribution is required and normal rules of decent living only are applied. (S)

138.Grimsby: b) **Haycroft Street Homes (Flottergate Benevolent Fund and Homes)**. The Benevolent Homes is a row of nine bungalow dwellings built in 1933 through a legacy of a Miss Atkin. Sir James Blindell, a Liberal MP for Holland-with-Boston, Methodist and Grimsby business man conceived the idea of the homes and led the Committee. There was substantial rebuilding and modernisation carried out in 1981. Preference is given to applicants from Haycroft Street chapel (now known as Laceby Road chapel). There is no resident warden but a warden is provided by the trust to look in on residents daily. The trustees state: *We can modestly claim that the provision and maintenance of the Benevolent Homes is an example of practical Christian work.* (S)

139.Grimsby: c) **Smedley Cottages**, (1902), Hainton Avenue, Sixhills Street. These are also run by the Grimsby Fishermen's group and include six flats known as the Joseph Cobley Houses. New two-bedroom semi-detached bungalows have been added to this group – six at New Waltham and three at Scartho. There are in addition 31 housing units belonging to the trust in Waltham. [See Waltham and Scartho entries]. (S)

140.Harlaxton: near Grantham. Swine Hill - this single-storey, coursed stone building with brick quoins and pantile roof, was once three cottages. The chimney stacks are at the gable ends with coped double octagonal flues. The building is probably one of those rebuilt c. 1770-1820 by George de Ligne Gregory and remodelled in picturesque style c. 1820-1840 by Gregory Gregory. It is now known as Bede Cottage. There is no record of the cottages being registered with the Charity Commissioners so it seems likely that they were used for old retainers of the Harlaxton estate and when the whole estate was sold by Major Pearson Gregory in 1937 the cottages were sold as one lot. It was listed in the Jackson Stops and Staff sale

Harlaxton: Bede Cottage, now a private house, was once three cottages forming part of the almshouses rebuilt in the late eighteenth century by George de Ligne Gregory.

catalogue as three cottages with about 14 poles of ground (less than half an acre in total). Each cottage had two rooms, pantry, outbuildings and garden. Two were let on monthly tenancies; one to a Miss Fisher, rent-free and one to a Mrs Butter at £3.8s per annum. The third was vacant at the time of the sale. The purchaser of the cottages had the right to draw water from the well on adjoining land. No mains services were in use at that time. A newspaper report stated that no tenant was dispossessed against his or her will. (P)

141.Heckington: 5 miles east of Sleaford; 11 miles west of Boston. Four almshouses on The Green erected in 1888 (Pevsner says 1886) bequeathed by **Henry Godson**. These are now converted into two houses. **Edward Godson**, brother of Henry, bequeathed four almshouse flats in Cameron Street erected 1904. The donors were gentlemen of

Heckington: The almshouse in Cameron Street was bequeathed by Edward Godson in 1904. Mr Mackinder, a resident of nineteen years, stands outside his flat.

independent means and bachelors. In 1974 the Charity Commissioners combined the two charities. At that date there was no money in the trust fund and an application was made to the District Council for grants and loans. This has now been repaid. Originally the accommodation was for widows and spinsters of good character but now men are also accommodated. Residents pay a maintenance contribution which includes heating costs in the case of the flats and water rates in the case of the houses. (S)

142.Holton le Moor: 3 miles southwest from Caistor: **Dixon Almshouses**. Mrs Amelia Margaretta Jameson Dixon left the residue of her estate to be devoted to the erection of almshouses in the parish in 1910. There are two bungalows in the middle of a terrace and a two-storey house on either side. The houses are brick-built with pantiled roofs and an iron fence and gates of the period at the front. There is a decorative dentillation on the gable ends and diamond-shaped chimneys. The builders were J Mills and C W Saunby. A central plaque reads: *'My song shall be always of the loving kindness of the lord. July 14 1910 Welbore Bp of Grantham Blessed these houses. Herein let steadfast love abide; May joy and peace dwell side by side; And whatsoever shall befall: God's spirit rule and lead you all. Aim ever life to lead aright; Make ready for God's cause to fight; Reject the ill, Approve the just; Armed each one soberly in trust; Duty to do in every day: And so excel in honour's way.'* This Edwardian exhortation, or warning, might have come from an earlier century – such

Horncastle: Whelpton's Almshouses were erected in 1861. Their founder, George Whelpton, had made a fortune from the manufacture of laxative pills.

wording would not be found in the second half of the twentieth century. (S)

143.Horncastle: Whelpton's Almshouses – four houses with an endowment of £6 yearly and two tons of coal each for four poor widows, inhabitants of the county of Lincoln. Good new porches added c. 1980. Another bequest by Ida Bowen, who died in 1981, enabled two adjacent terraced houses to be added to the trust. A loan for repairs and up-dating was obtained about this time from the Housing Corporation which is a central Government body set up to deal with housing matters. A plaque on the houses in Queen Street reads: *These six almshouses were erected by George Whelpton Albert Road Regents Park London AD 1861 In memory of his late wife Elizabeth who died December 11 1858;* Plaques over two porches read: *The porches were erected in 1983 with a generous bequest from Ida Bowen.* George Whelpton, who was a member of the Warrenite chapel in Louth, made a fortune by manufacturing laxative pills. (S)

144.Keadby: near Crowle (date unknown). The Charity Commissioners, in 1837, stated that an almshouse probably once belonging to William Dixon had fallen down. A new house was erected by the parish with a gift of £71.10s received from Messrs Glen. The two acres of land left by Dixon by way of endowment was exchanged for 17½ acres at enclosure and increased in value due to the warping process. Kelly's Directory of 1905 states that the Dixon charity was, at that date, distributed in money. (X)

Kirmington: Four almshouses were erected by the Earl of Yarborough in 1888. They are still part of the Yarborough estate but are no longer almshouses.

145.Kirmington: in Brigg/Caistor/Grimsby triangle. Four almshouses were erected by the Earl of Yarborough in 1888, at the same time as a school, at a cost of £800. Both buildings stand north of the church. They are still administered by Lord Yarborough's agent but are no longer almshouses. (P)

146.Kirton in Holland: 4 miles from Boston - Four almshouses bequeathed by **John Speak** in 1928. John Speak was the head of a Yorkshire spinning firm. (b.1844 - d 1931) In August 1928 he laid the foundation stone to the cottages. The foundation stone inscription reads: *These cottage homes were built by John Speak, The Grange, Kirton. AD 1928 in thankfulness to God for His many mercies.* Provision is for four widows or spinsters of good character. Speak left £522,000 in his will which included the bequest and land conveyed to the trustees for the upkeep. Now called **Kirton Consolidated Charities** incorporating **Hunt's Charity** and **Speak Cottage Homes**. (S)

147.Lea: near Gainsborough. **Lea Almshouses**, for the use of two women, were bequeathed by Miss Frances Olive Anderson in 1916 and invested in the diocese of Lincoln. The Rector and churchwardens were trustees. When Lea Hall was occupied the maintenance of the houses was covered by the Hall workmen. When the Hall was sold the maintenance costs fell on the trustees but not on the funds of Lea Church. The only income was a small amount from Lea Charities Fund started by Miss Frances Olive Anderson. Schemes were drawn up in the mid-twentieth century to obtain grants for the houses but these failed and an order was made for their demolition by the Rural Council. When a new estate was planned (1960s) the developers of the land (Thornhill) and the owners of the houses (the Diocese) made an agreement that the houses should be demolished and the unused portions of the ground was incorporated into the churchyard. In 1967/8 two semi-detached bungalows were built on land exchanged for the original site. Poor, aged or infirm persons selected by the management committee, preferably, but not exclusively, members of the C of E and residents of Lea are eligible to live there. (S)

148.Leasingham: 2 miles northwest of Sleaford: a) **Bishop of Nottingham's Almshouses** were endowed by Edward Trollope in 1885 for the use of aged or infirm members of the Church of England and now consist of three flats in the original building in Lincoln Road. The Endowment Fund consists of Consolidated stock and reinvested stock (by Order of the Charity Commissioners 1951). The trustees of this charity are common to those of the Walter Wright Almshouse Charity and they hold joint meetings. (S)

149.Leasingham: b) **Walter Wright's Almshouse Charity** now consists of two adjoining bungalows typical of the time in St Andrew's Crescent. It was founded in 1967 by the will of Walter Wright. Provision is for poor persons who have at any time resided in the parish of Leasingham for a period of not less than five years. (S)

150.Legbourne: 3 miles southeast from Louth: **John Gainsborough Bede House Trust** - two semi-detached bungalows on Station Road built 1924, one for Legbourne, one for Little Cawthorpe. (S)

Lincoln: At St Anne's Bedehouse, each house is named after one of the parishes from which candidates were eligible to apply. The initials RWS refer to the founder, Richard Waldo Sibthorp.

151.Lincoln: St Anne's Bedehouses, Sewell Road – Fourteen houses paid for by Revd Richard Waldo Sibthorp, in 1847 (but probably not completed until the 1860s) by builder George Myers to a design by A W N Pugin. The chapel and wellhouse were built in the 1850s by Charles Ward to a design by William Butterfield. The houses were intended as residences for fourteen females of limited means with two rooms, a convenient scullery and back yard. The allowance to each inmate was 5/6d per week in 1905 with three doles of 7/- each, 10/- in clothes, 2½ tons of coals annually and a new cloak every fifth year. Myers and Pugin were both very much concerned with the Great Exhibition of 1851 and were prize-winners at the event. Myers was the inventor of a patented machine for cutting Gothic tracery and mouldings and any circular form in wood or stone. The stonework on the doorways and windows is witness to Myer's machine's capabilities. The houses are of brick with blue clay Staffordshire tiled roofs with crocheted ridge tiles. Mr R Lucas, the builder who refurbished the houses in 1994, reported that all the original work was of a high quality and the builder had been generous with substantial timber for the roof trusses. Blue Staffordshire clay tiles for the roofs were matched and replaced where necessary and chimneys which had been taken down in a previous modernisation were replaced with stone and brick, the stone being supplied and cut by masons at Rattee and Kett of Cambridge. The bricks would have been obtained locally as there were many brickworks in the district. The almswomen used to have to be committed members of the Church of England (their

Lincoln: Some later almshouse foundations incorporated chapels within or adjacent to their buildings. St Anne's Bedehouse in Lincoln has a detached chapel designed in the 1850s by William Butterfield.

founder swung from Canterbury to Rome and back) but although attendance at chapel is preferred, it is not now compulsory. The residents currently make a realistic contribution to the maintenance costs; the age of entry has been lowered to 55 and applications are sought nationwide. The original warden's house, once occupied by Father R W Sibthorp the founder as warden, has now been sold; one house is maintained as a guesthouse for residents' visitors and two cottages (now one) built at a later date are occupied by a married couple caretaker/ warden. Income from the sale of the warden's house in 1995 was used, with a grant from English Heritage, to renovate the chimneys of the houses and the chapel roof. The orchard has also been sold and is now the garden of a separate house but the residents maintain a right to pick spring flowers therein. The lowering of the age for admission and the vigour of modern women living there now is illustrated by a resident, Mary Downey, who was a joiner and has fitted her own kitchen with wooden units. The chapel and graveyard are incorporated in the grounds and, although there is no space left for interments, ashes can still be scattered there. There are currently (2002) two men amongst the residents. (S)

152.Long Sutton: near Norfolk: a) Consolidated Charities incorporating Tilson's charity (no date) derived from 15 acres of land endowed almshouses for four poor widows; **Gee's almshouses** and **Winfrey Almshouses**. There are two pairs of brick bungalows; Gee's which are bedsitters plus kitchen and bathroom built 1913 from a bequest by Emma Gee who died in 1911 and Winfrey's built 1925 which have a bedroom and sitting room. The latter were built from an endowment by Ann Winfrey. A plaque on these two bungalows reads: '*To brighten the sunset of life for the occupants*'. (X)

153.Long Sutton: b) **Sowter's charity** was derived from 6½ acres of land and three cottages – the rent of one cottage going to the maintenance of two widows in the others. There is no longer a cottage but the charity still exists to provide a pension for poor widows. (X)

154.Louth: a) Orme Almshouses built in 1885. The Revd Frederick Orme MA, rector of Lyndon, Rutland, erected ten almshouses with a porter's lodge for ten poor men on the site of the old prison, at the junction of Eastgate and Ramsgate. He endowed them with £7,200 invested in stocks, the joint income was to be used for repairs and insurance and providing the pensioners with a 'long coat with a big button with a dolphin thereon' every four years for weekday use, an extra coat for Sunday and, once in six years, a tall beaver hat. The pensioners were to be paid 5s a week and the Lodge-Keeper (to be a married man without resident children) 15s a week. The buildings, designed by James Fowler, are of red brick with stone dressings in a Jacobean style and stand in an ornamental acre of ground. The almshouses were built on the site of the House of Correction and the following anecdote was told to me by Dorothy King of Spilsby. 'My mother, Mrs Susanna King (née Broadley) who was born in 1868 said that she remembered being taken for a walk by her father who lifted her on his shoulders to see the men on the treadmill in the prison grounds. She saw a man try to pick up a fallen pear from the ground and he was whipped there and then.' The pear tree still stands in the grounds of the almshouses and still bears fruit. In 1995 a new pear tree was planted beside the old one. The residents are still male. The accommodation, which is centrally-heated, comprises a bed-sitting room, bathroom and galley kitchen. There is no warden at present. (S)

155.Louth: b) **Ayscough Trust**, 65 – 71 Kidgate – from a bequest by Alice Hannah Ayscough - four flats opened in 1984 for people of little means who do not own a house. (S)

156.Market Deeping – near the Northamptonshire border – Church Street. Miss Mary Ann Scotney gave by will several sums for the founding and endowment of six almshouses for the reception of six Protestant women, being either unmarried or widows, without families, to be chosen by the trustees – three to be residents of Market Deeping, one from Deeping St James, one from Thornhaugh and another from Werrington. The houses were built of stone in 1876/7 at a cost of £2,100 from a design by Edward Browning of Stamford and form three sides of a square on a site given by Miss Scotney in her lifetime. There was an endowment in consolidated funds. There was a spacious washhouse for the common use of the inmates. There were to be eight trustees; four to be Church of England and four of the Calvinistic Dissenting faith. Anyone who was in direct line from the donor was to have preference of residence. Each woman received £2.2s. annually in 1905. The houses were modernised in 1963 and a further bequest from the Miss Stangers was used to install indoor lavatories. Now the residents are still single or widowed women and a maintenance contribution is payable. (S)

157.Market Rasen: Catholic almshouses were erected in 1845 on the main road, from a bequest by David Young of Market Rasen who died in 1832. There was an endowment of £20 yearly to each of three inmates who also lived rent-free. The last resident was Mr Patrick Lavell who died c. 1992. The house was sold and is now occupied privately. It is called ***Young's Cottage*** after the founder. (P)

158.Nettleton: near Caistor. **Nettleton Memorial Cottages** founded 1922 as a memorial to men who had fallen during the First World War. The initial idea came from Sir Culling Eardley and money was raised by public subscription. The opening was performed by Lord and Lady Yarborough. The house was described as 'a splendidly designed parlour cottage, self-contained, with scullery, pantry, a good-sized living room, two bedrooms. It is built of red stock bricks with cavity walls, corner stones and slated roof'. It was intended for an aged couple, residents of Nettleton. (S)

159.Nocton (date unknown) 7 miles southeast of Lincoln. Almshouses were given by Frederick Robinson, first Earl of Ripon, (1783-1859) of Nocton Hall in his lifetime. He was the only male Prime Minister that Lincolnshire has produced. The four cottages continued to be supported by Robinson's son George, Marquis of Ripon. The 1881 census returns state that Emma Scoley, widow, 69, was a resident. By 1891 the cottages were no longer used as almshouses but had become estate cottages. These houses stand near the Hall gates on Main Street and are known as Ripon Row. A directory of 1856 states that there were four cottages in Nocton for the free use of poor families. There is, also, a stone cottage with tiled roof with an 1833 date-stone on the corner of Wellhead Lane and Main Street which was known as the almshouse although it was not used as such in living memory. This building became the Post Office and is now in private hands. (P)

160.North Thoresby: called **Frederick Field and Lords Trust**: it holds **Askew's Almshouses** in the Trust. The present buildings are four dwellings, built in 1935 and known as the **Jubilee Cottages**. They each comprise of a living room; kitchen; pantry; bathroom two bedrooms; outside toilet; coalhouse and washhouse and good garden. The trustees try to keep to precise terms of the will of Fred Askew but this is not always possible so any deserving case in the village is considered. Fred Askew was a North Thoresby parish councillor and JP who had the cottages built in his lifetime. Married but childless Mr Askew was a baker who owned the general stores and bakery in the village. His will, of 1958, directed that the Charity Managers should not exclude 'any person on the ground of religion but give preference so far as may be to applicants who have lived in the parish not less than ten consecutive years and to agricultural labourers or other persons engaged in agricultural pursuits.' All residents were to be of pensionable age and a minimum rent of 2/- (10p) per week could be imposed by the Managers. (S)

161.Old Leake: near Boston. a) **Harlocks' Cottages** – founded in 1958 by W H Harlock and Ethel Harlock this charity also incorporates the **Swineshead Almshouse Charity**. There are six semi-detached bungalows built, in 1960/1, in a crescent formation with lawn and gardens to the front and a small private garden to the rear; each unit has sitting room, two bedrooms, kitchen and bathroom. They are for the use of 'poor persons of good character who from old age or infirmity are deserving objects of the charity'. They must have lived in the parish for more than five years. (S)

162.Old Leake: near Boston. b) **Alenson and Erskine Almshouse Charity**: two pre-war bungalows and two post-war bungalows for retired people of the parish. (S)

163.Owston Ferry: Isle of Axholme – built and endowed by Miss Frances Sanders in 1860 for six aged females of good character, being members of the Church of England who had resided in the Archdeaconry of Stow for at least two years. The early residents were expected to attend the parish church and were to help with fruit picking, probably at Trent Hall, North Street, the home of the Sanders' family. The original houses had a bedroom with small fire-grate, a living room with a black Yorkshire-style cooking range and a small scullery. Above the range was stone lintel on which was inscribed one of the Beatitudes. The houses, which are listed Grade II, present an attractive, brick-built, row with stone mullioned windows and decorative stone door frames. The roof has hexagonal slates and multi-sided chimney pots. Atop the buildings, on the central gable is a statue of a woman reading a bible. During the Second World War soldiers were billeted in one of the almshouses and were said to be well looked after by the residents of the other houses. Now there is no necessity to belong to the Church of England and most residents do not have local roots. Residents have to be over 60. A small rent charge is made. (S)

Ruskington: The Teetotal Houses, built in 1887, incorporate the word 'TEETOTAL' in their ornate stonework.

164. Riby: built in 1848 for four poor men each of whom received £9 twice yearly, by Colonel G Tomline, grandson of Dr George (Pretyman) Tomline, Bishop of Lincoln 1787-1820. Demolished in the late 1970s in spite of being listed. (X)

165. Ruskington: a) **Teetotal Houses**, Jubilee Street. Built 1887 and placed in the hands of the trustees for the benefit of the poor of Ruskington for ever. The houses still exist but the running of them was taken over by the Longhurst Housing Association in the mid 1990s together with the **Scott Houses** (below). (S)

166. Ruskington: b) **J R Scott**, 1904. Four houses in Priory Road now Longhurst Housing Association houses. (S)

167. Scartho: a) Lavenham Road, Conniston Avenue and Westbourne Grove. Four Smedley Cottages (see Waltham) were acquired in 2000 by The Grimsby and District Homes for Poor and Aged Workers in the Fish Trade.

168. Scartho: b) **Grantham's Almshouses** – founded *c.* 1930: three blocks of two semi-detached bungalows built in the early 1930s under the will of Joseph Grantham. The cottages were furnished and inhabitants received 10/- and a bag of coal per week. They are for 'persons in need, being not less than 60 years of age and resident in the area comprising the parishes of Bradley and Irby and the area of the former parish of Scartho'. The houses were modernised *c.* 1985. (S)

169.Sibsey: near Boston. Frithville Road. This almshouse was recorded in 1956 by a member of the Business and Professional Women's Association during a survey but no trace can now be found and there is no memory of it amongst present village inhabitants. (S)

170.Sleaford: Jessie Snow's Almshouses in Westgate Sleaford were founded in 1952. Built as three bungalows; now two exist and continue as almshouses. Residents are to be needy women, whether aged or not, who

Spalding: Kingston Cottage Homes – Four houses were built in 1907 in an ornamental Edwardian 'institutional' style.

are resident in the parish of Sleaford at the time of appointment. (S)

171.Spalding: Charity known as **Spalding Town Husbands** incorporates: a) **Kingston Cottage Homes** designed by J B Corby and built in 1907 on South Parade. Four houses were built by Siddons and Freemantle of Oundle at a cost of £1648. The style is ornamental, institutional Edwardian in red brick with fish-scale clay tiles on the roof and Elizabethan-type chimney pots. There were 100 applicants for four houses when the houses were built. A further endowment of land (21 acres) was made by the founder's nephew a year after Samuel Kingston's death in 1905. (S)

172.Spalding: b) **Dalton Homes**; two bungalows were built in 1938 by the **Edwin Dalton Almshouse Charity** in West Parade. Edwin Dalton owned a furniture shop in Spalding. The plaque states that the houses were built and endowed ' to the glory of God'. Spalding Town Husbands took over the management of these houses in the 1990s. (S)

173.Spalding: c) **Dr Adrian Gall Homes;** sixteen almshouses were built in 1971 on land off Clay Lake Lane which was formerly a railway line (axed by Dr Beeching in the 1960s). The brick bungalows were designed by Desmond Aite of King's Lynn and were erected with money raised by public subscription. (S)

174.Spalding: d) **William and Elizabeth Masham Almshouses**; These six bungalows were endowed and built in the founders' lifetimes in 1960. William Masham was a Spalding

Spalding: Sixteen almshouses, known as the Adrian Gall Homes, were built in 1971 on a disused railway line. In common with the rest of this town's generous provision of almshouses, they are administered by the Spalding Town Husbands.

builder who had previously built six Council bungalows on an adjoining site on Green Lane. They are brick bungalows, typical of their date, with concrete roof tiles and concrete moulded guttering and metal framed windows. The last two features are giving some trouble and will eventually be replaced. (S)

175.Spalding: e) **Van Geest Homes**; Fourteen attractive brick bungalows were built round three sides of a square in Hoekman Way with easily maintained gardens in front. These have gables and porches over the front doors and are less flat and dull than bungalows built a decade or two earlier. Lucille and John Van Geest gave £250,000 for the building of the houses which were opened in 1994 in their lifetime. (S)

Spalding: The Van Geest Homes in Hoekman Way comprise fourteen attractive and easily maintained bungalows set around three sides of a square.

176.Spalding: f) **Alice Wilson Homes**: Six almshouses were built in 1981 endowed by Alice Wilson but managed from the start by the Town Husbands. The architects were Ruddle Wilkinson and the builder was F Parker. The cost was £126,325. Mrs Wilson was the widow of the editor of the Free Press in Spalding. The Town Husbands subsequently made a decision to build four flats in front of these houses in Winsover Road in 1989 but the plan did not come to fruition. (S)

177.Spilsby: John Coley Trust founded 1949. Eight brick bungalows built *c.* 1952 for pensioners who must have lived in Spilsby, Toynton, Hundleby or Raithby for five years. Residents live rent and rates free. John Coley was a farmer and licensee of the Nelson Inn in Spilsby. He left sufficient land for the trust's maintenance. (S)

178.Stamford: **Fryer's Callis**, Kettering Road; These houses were built in 1832 to the designs of George Basevi. They are of coursed rubble with freestone dressings. The houses were built at the bequest of Henry Fryer but they contain mullioned panels as follows: a) Thomas Truesdale insig; b) arms of Fryer and crest of Hurst inscribed *Hen Fryer Fundatoris insig* and *laboci Hurst Benafactoris insig:* c) arms of Burghley. (S)

179.Sturton by Stow: The Charity Commissioners' Report of 1837 stated that there was an almshouse with half an acre of land attached which had been used by four poor people rent free from time immemorial – but there was no means of ascertaining the origin. The rent, in 1837, was paid from the Poor Rates. White's Directory (1872) noted that the house had recently fallen into decay. (X)

180.Surfleet: **Surfleet Cottage Homes**. Four bungalows on Newlands Road run by Surfleet United Charities. This group was founded in 1912 when the houses were built. It incorporates the Joseph Burton endowment and three other charities; also a land endowment from Samuel Elsdale which still generates a rent income. The houses were originally for widows but now any elderly resident of Surfleet is eligible. (S)

181.Tathwell: Eric and Betty West Almshouses; 1973. This is a detached bungalow for old and incapacitated persons being (as far as possible) residents in the parish of Tathwell. (S)

182.Thorganby: Village Houses founded 1966 by Mrs Margaret Manby and Mrs May Cresswell who conceived the idea of two houses in the old school and school house. The school was built in 1868 by the third Earl of Yarborough and is of local brick with pantiled roof. The two storeyed school house which adjoins the school is home to one resident and the school is converted into a ground-floor residence. The conversion was done by Staines Bros. of Louth. Both founders died within two years of the conversion so the trustees had to pay over £1000 in estate duty. Preference is given to retired farm workers who have lived locally but, as the village has no bus or shop, occupants need to be able to drive or have

Thorganby: The 'Village Houses' were founded in 1966 using the disused Victorian (1868) school and its school house. Preference is given to retired farm-workers who have lived locally, although young people in need of housing may now also be considered.

Thurlby: Ann Elizabeth Mason founded almshouses for five people in 1953, on The Green, in memory of her mother, Mary Adcock, and uncle, Samuel Harvey. (right) Three more bungalows (above) were built in 1965 on additional land on Crown Lane given by Tom and Harry Fairchild.

someone to take them shopping. As there are very few farm workers a much wider catchment area is now accepted and young people would be considered if necessary rather than have an almshouse empty. (S)

183.Thurlby: **Ann Elizabeth Mason Charity**, Crown Lane and The Green, founded in 1953 consisting of two groups of post-war brick bungalows (five units in total). They were founded by Mrs Ann Elizabeth Mason in memory of her mother, Mary Ann Adcock and her uncle Samuel Spencer Harvey for senior citizens who have lived in Thurlby parish for at least ten years. An additional gift of land was made in 1965 by Tom and Harry Fairchild and with the proceeds of this land the Crown Lane land was purchased and a further three bungalows were built. Ann Mason, who lived at Thurlby Post Office, also left a capital sum of money for four widows. This charity has now been amalgamated with the almshouse one and gift parcels are distributed at Christmas. The houses were endowed with 20 acres of tenanted land at Thurlby Fen and other income is obtained from deposits in equities and bonds *etc.* (S)

184.Waltham: Smedley Cottages, Manor Drive; Leas Close: this group of 26 dwellings comes under the aegis of The Grimsby and District Homes for Poor and Aged Workers Fish Trade (Smedley Cottages). They were opened in 1938 and modernised in 1982. The founder, Captain W H Smedley MBE was brought up in Sheffield and ran away to sea at the age of 14. He rose to be a skipper and was later made the Port Missioner in Grimsby. By his initiative he raised money from ship owners and first bought a plot in Waltham. The houses are for retired men, couples or widows who have been employed in the fish trade. (S)

185.Weston: near Spalding: Consolidated Charity was formed in 1969 by the amalgamation of eighteen small local charities (seventeen of them formed pre-1837). The old houses were demolished and two one-bedroomed bungalows were built for the use of local residents (single or couple) who were in need, hardship or distress. Some allotments belonging to an old charity were sold but allotments still generate a small income for the new charity. The oldest of the small charities amalgamated in this village was the **Harrox Charity** which arose from a donation of land by John Harrox in 1560. About 1809 a man called Desborough enclosed part of this land from waste and built a house on it but, from 1813, he paid

30/- per annum to the feoffees or trustees of the charity. In 1817 the payments ceased and the house became the property of the trustees. (S)

186.Winterton: between Scunthorpe and Barrow on Humber. **Miss Mary Clark Almshouse Trust** founded and built in 1904 in the founder's lifetime. £660 was left for the erection of the buildings and £2,045.9s.9d. for future maintenance and the payment of 5/- per week to each resident. Miss Clark kept a draper's shop in the village. Three brick and pantile bungalows were erected for poor unmarried applicants of good character over 60 years of age who had lived in the parish for two years. The trustees are now flexible as to applicants in need. The *ex-officio* chairmanship of trustees is always held by the vicar. (S)

187. Withern: Annie Pahud foundation; 1907. Three brick terraced houses on Chalk Lane were purpose built. They consist of two rooms and kitchen and bathroom. Another house was left as an endowment by Mr Pahud who was a Louth schoolmaster. This latter house has now been sold to provide a pool of funds. Residents were originally to be from the parish of Withern. The trustees are now more flexible and there is no age limit for applicants. (S)

188.Wyberton: **Cooke-Yarborough Almshouses Trust** in Tytton Lane. The inscription reads: *Two cottages built in memory of Arthur Cooke-Yarborough and his family Resident in Wyberton 1879-1965.* (S)

Wyberton: Two cottages were built in Tytton Lane to the memory of Arthur Cooke-Yarborough, a Wyberton resident from 1879 to 1965

A Legacy of Almshouse Building

by Paula Judson

We have seen how the almshouse tradition has continued over the centuries, and how buildings for the relief of the poor developed from the monastic houses, to institutions and then became more domestic in their appearance.

Almshouses vary widely in their forms and styles, from grand architectural compositions to homely cottages. I would like to take a closer look at the surviving almshouse buildings in Lincolnshire, the different building forms and architectural styles. This chapter identifies common characteristics as well as some of the more unusual features found in Lincolnshire almshouses.

Although not the earliest, **Browne's Hospital** (1494) in Stamford (*pg 10 & 11*) is described[1] as 'one of the best surviving medieval almshouses in England' and the only remaining example of the infirmary hall arrangement in Lincolnshire. The plan is derived from the early medieval hospitals which had a single large room with cubicles for the inmates along the sides and a chapel at the eastern end. The main block is two storeys with cubicles on the dimly lit ground floor. The rooms were spartan; in 1731 the small rooms were furnished with only a bed, a shelf, candlestick and extinguisher; by 1766 hospital records indicate that most rooms had acquired a second shelf and cupboard. The buildings were altered and enlarged in the nineteenth century and the cubicles removed.

The **Lord Burghley's Hospital, Stamford** (*pg 41*) is a rehabilitation of an older decayed establishment dating from the twelfth century. The range of lodgings built in 1616 survives, although much altered. In the original building there was on the ground floor a long corridor with ten rooms opening off it (*see plan below*). This feature of an internal passage giving access to the rooms is found only occasionally in almshouses, a nearby example being the *Maison Dieu* of 1640 at Melton Mowbray, Leicestershire.

The period following the dissolution of the religious houses under Henry VIII produced a great many foundations. This also marked a change from the monastic hospital to a more permanent residential form of accommodation. In sixteenth and seventeenth centuries a great many new institutions were formed, including colleges, universities, hospitals and almshouses. Many adopted the courtyard or quadrangle design (enclosed on all four sides), or the open quadrangle (*i.e.* enclosed by buildings on three sides and open on one side). This arrangement continued to be used in later almshouse building.

Most almshouses endowed by wealthy benefactors or commissioned by charitable institutions were purpose-built to house the poor, although a few are conversions from pre-existing buildings, such as the former **Williamson's Callis, Stamford** *(pg 41)* which dates from the early seventeenth century and was adapted to accommodate six poor widows in 1770.

The row of almshouses at **Tattershall** (*pg 21*) date from the early seventeenth century and are in the vernacular tradition, built with readily available materials, in this case re-used limestone and brick. The building has a pantiled roof but would probably have been thatched. An archaeological survey carried out in 1997 revealed that the building was originally ten dwellings and followed the post-medieval pattern of single room lodgings, each entered from the outside. The almshouses were converted into five dwellings in the 1960s and refurbished in 1995.

Middlecotts Hospital, Fosdyke near Holbeach (*pg 31*) is another example of a simple vernacular building dating from the early seventeenth century. An attractive, if plain, row built of brick. The pantiled roof was probably originally

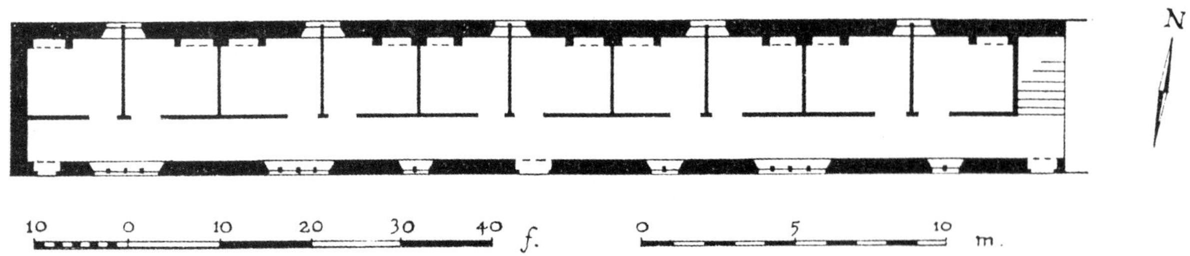

A reconstruction drawing of the layout of Lord Burghley's Hospital of 1616. © Crown copyright NMR

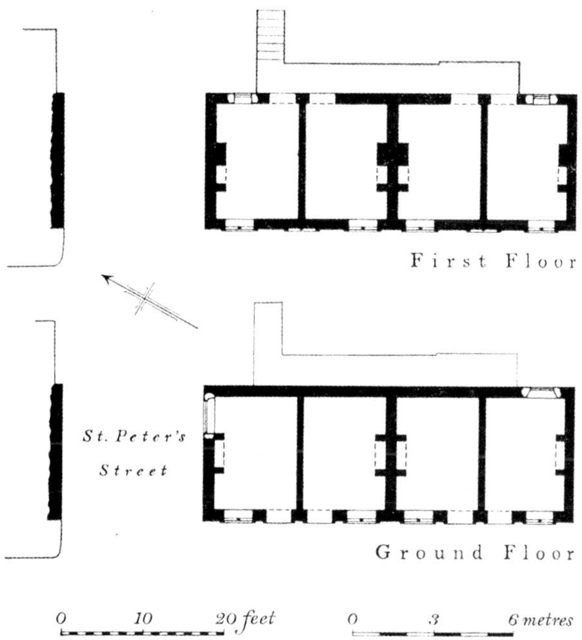

Hopkin's Hospital in Stamford has two storeys with access to the first floor rooms from an open terrace at the rear. © Crown copyright NMR

thatched. It has horizontal 'Yorkshire' sliding sash windows with small panes.

Other noteworthy examples from this period include **Worlaby Hospital** (1663) near Brigg and the almshouses at **Langton by Horncastle** (1690). Both display Artisan Mannerism, a style of brickwork peculiar to the eastern counties of England.

A number of Lincolnshire almshouses take the form of a terraced row - this arrangement was cheaper to construct than individual cottages. Accommodation was usually provided on one or two levels. Single storey accommodation offers obvious advantages to the elderly or infirm. Building on two storeys could be due to restrictions on the size of the site and the need to maximise the number of units of accommodation. Sometimes the different sexes were accommodated on separate floors. **Hopkins Hospital**, Stamford, (*see plan left*) is two storeys, with access to the first floor rooms from an open terrace at the rear. Each floor had four rooms which were entered separately; access to the first floor rooms was from the terrace (east side) and access to the ground floor was from the west side. **St Peter's Callis**, Stamford, rebuilt in 1863, was in the early nineteenth century a building with lodgings on two levels, the upper reached by an external stone staircase and a covered timber gallery on the rear or south elevation.

The dwellings were intended primarily to meet residents' basic physical needs – shelter, heat, food, and sometimes clothing was provided. However, their spiritual needs were not neglected and many almshouses had their own chapel attached including **Browne's Hospital, Lord Burghley's Bedehouses**, **Carre's Hospital, Eastgate, Sleaford** (*pg 38*) The detached chapel was a later form of development, as at **St Anne's Bedehouses, Lincoln** (*pg 60*) which was designed by William Butterfield, a well-known nineteenth century architect who designed many other church buildings including the chapel at Keble College, Oxford.

Although basic by today's standards, the accommodation provided by almshouses was probably far better than that endured by the majority of the population. The individual dwellings were intended to accommodate one or two people, usually elderly residents. Occupants included retired farm labourers or estate workers, clergy, widows and other 'deserving poor'. The scale and simple treatment, however, reflected the humble social position of the occupants. The traditional almshouse accommodation was generally modest in size and consisted of just one or two rooms, a living room with sleeping lobby, and perhaps a separate pantry or larder.

In the eighteenth century the classical style predominated with strong symmetry, order and formality being the guiding principles. Georgian almshouses were modest in size and scale compared to their predecessors, and well-proportioned as might be expected in this age of elegance. There are few surviving examples in Lincolnshire.

Handcock's Hospital, Bardney (1712) (*pg 28*) is a substantial two-storey block with central projecting pediment, constructed in brick with ashlar dressings and horizontal string course. The building has an institutional appearance.

The almshouses at **Hemingby,** near Horncastle (*pg 33*) date from 1727 and performed a dual purpose. Originally built as four two-storey cottages and a school, on the edge of the churchyard, the building is now three dwellings.

By the late eighteenth century formal Classicism was falling out of favour and the Picturesque – with its emphasis on nature and disorder – became popular. The expressions of the Picturesque style included, variety and play of outline, asymmetrical positioning of buildings, porches, intricate detailing, overhanging eaves, recessed windows and large elaborate chimneys. Pattern books such as those produced by Nathaniel Kent (1775) and

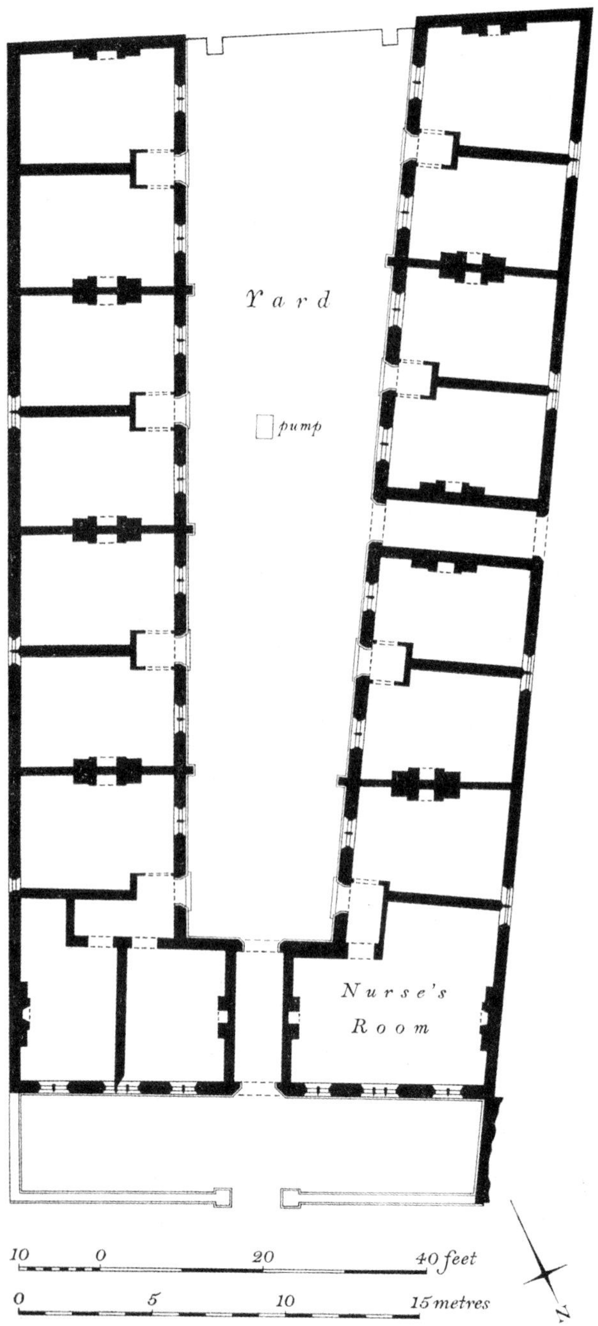

Truesdale's Hospital (left) is set around a yard with communal pump, while the inhabitants of Snowden's Hospital (right) share a garden.

© Crown copyright NMR

John Woods (1781) introduced new standards of living, and improvements in comfort and amenities, and these were transferred to houses for the poor.

The nineteenth century was 'the age of philanthropy' and this is evident in the numbers of almshouses built and rebuilt during this period. There are some notable examples in Lincolnshire. Many almshouses are built around a communal courtyard or garden which allowed for sharing of facilities such as a well and outside 'privy'. Examples include the bedehouse at **Belton**, *(pg 24)* **Dawson's Almshouses** in **Grantham** *(pg 56)*, **Snowden's and Truesdale's, Stamford** *(see plans, left and right)*, and **Turnor's, Wragby** *(pg 43)*. Almshouses of this period belong to the 'polite' tradition rather than the vernacular, with buildings designed by architects, often using 'imported' materials such as Welsh slate which had to be transported long distances. Styles and features were borrowed from grand architecture. Pattern books such as John Loudon's *Encyclopaedia of Cottage, Farm and Villa Architecture and Furniture* (1833) were popular and influenced the design of almshouses. The effect of all these different ideas was a great variety of building styles. Some almshouses are quite plain with no more than a little decoration, whilst others, such as the **Teetotal Almshouses** in **Ruskington** *(pg 63)* stand out for their elaborate decoration. The extravagant ornamentation which includes moulded brickwork and foliate carving is typical of the late nineteenth century but seems almost frivolous – and could be regarded as out of place on a building that houses the poor.

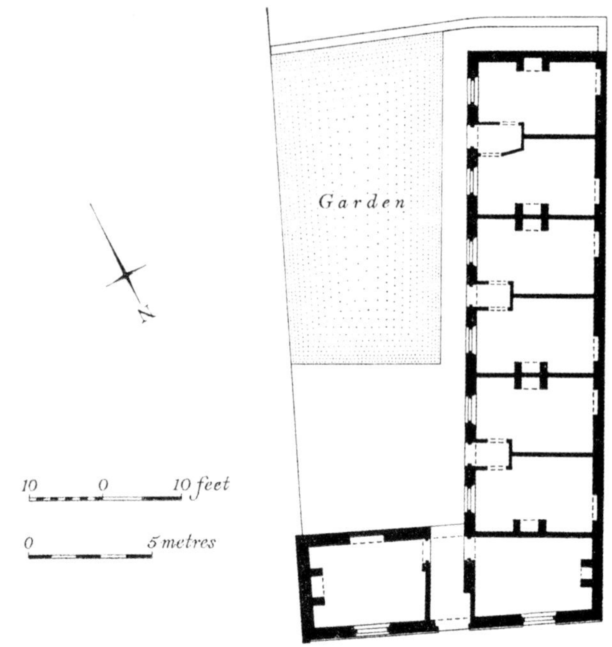

Some almshouses are built of costly materials by craftsmen accustomed to working on grand and lavish buildings, and a close attention to detail is evident. **St Anne's Bedehouses** in **Lincoln** *(pg 49)* (1847) were designed by AW Pugin, the great Gothic architect, for Richard Waldo Sibthorp, to house 13 gentlewomen. The work was carried out by the Hull born builder, George Myers. The buildings are of the highest quality, built of brick with stone dressings; the circular chimney stacks tower above the sweeping tiled roofs. Internally, the accommodation is all on one level and each unit comprises an entrance lobby, living room, bedroom, bathroom and kitchen.

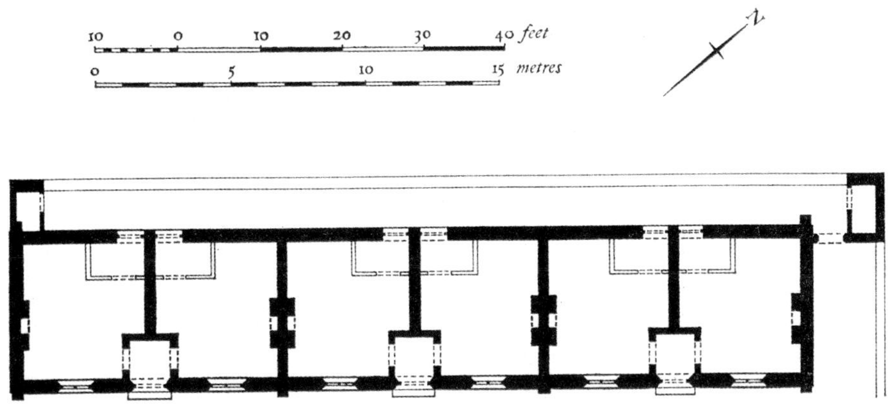

Fryer's Callis by architect George Basevi shows a very similar internal layout to Truesdale's Hospital (pg 69) also by Basevi. © Crown copyright NMR

Designs were often a repetition of similar buildings within a group. This is illustrated by **Fryer's Callis** *(see plan above)* and **Truesdale's Hospital** *(see plan pg 70)* in **Stamford** which were both built to designs by George Basevi and date from around the same time (c. 1832/33). Although there are variations in the detailing, there are similarities in the layout and form. The buildings are single storey, laid out in a long row (arranged along a narrow courtyard at Truesdale's), the dwellings are arranged in pairs with each pair subdivided by buttresses. Each unit has a central doorway with shared lobby. The rooms are of similar size, about 15ft by 18 ft with fireplace on the party wall. Both almshouses have been altered to provide improved accommodation.

The bedehouse at **Belton** dates from 1827 and is an attractive building in the estate style *i.e.* the architectural style is part of the 'corporate identity' of the estate. The almshouse, with its ashlar walls and slate roof, is constructed around three sides of an open quadrangle, the front courtyard is enclosed by an arcaded screen wall and gate. The almshouses at **Market Deeping** (*pg 48*) date from 1876/7 and are very similar in form.

The almshouses at **Wragby** (1840) (*pg 43*) were built around an open quadrangle with a garden area at the front. The building, which is in a Gothic style, provides ten units of self-contained accommodation, on two storeys. The accommodation is very generous; on the ground floor there is a lobby, kitchen, living room, understairs cupboard (converted to a w.c.). On the first floor there is a good-sized bedroom and bathroom. Units 5, 6 and 7 have all been extended and have an additional bedroom.

The romantic image of the almshouse endures and is epitomised by the **Orme Almshouses** (*pg 45*) (1885) in **Louth** by James Fowler, and the **Henry Godson Almshouses** in **Heckington** *(pg 47)*, built in 1886. This idyllic row of four cottages on the village green were built of red brick in a restrained Gothic style. The building has been converted into two dwellings but retains its original features, including the white-painted metal lancet casement windows with small diamond lattice panes, and a front canopy. The almshouses in **Cameron Street** *(pg 58)* are almost identical to those on the Green, although built some 30 years later by Edward Godson. This building which was altered in 1974 and is now four maisonettes has, sadly, lost some of its charm. The chimneys, front canopy, and two front doors are gone, and the roof slates have been replaced by concrete tiles.

Brick is a favoured building material in the east of the county. Stone occurs only in the west of the county, and is the dominant building material in Stamford. Brick is easy to use compared to stone (which has to be dressed) and more economical, although stone dressings are often used as a feature. Lincolnshire has a tradition of mud building but this type of construction is associated with the meanest of building so is not favoured for almshouses. Pantile and slate was used extensively for roofing (and often replaced an earlier covering of thatch). Stone tile and plain tile is occasionally seen.

Towards the end of the nineteenth century and into the twentieth century, there were improvements in heating, better ventilation and lighting, and the importance of the external appearance over internal convenience of occupiers was fading.

In the early twentieth century, the Garden City and Arts and Crafts movements promoted the building of cottages with wide frontages, good-sized front and rear gardens, good natural daylight and sunlight, improved ventilation and health for occupiers. Long uniform terraces were seen as monotonous and undesirable, as was arbitrary and unnecessary ornamentation. Instead, subtlety of colour and texture in materials, and sweeping rooflines with dormers or hipped roofs were used to add interest. Internally, the trend was towards larger floor areas, more rooms and better services. Compare the **Fishermans Almshouses** (1896) (*pg 47*) in **Grimsby** with the **Horton Almshouses** (1908), **Boston** (*pg 52*).

The almshouses at **Aylesby** (*pg 46*) date from 1925. Pevsner describes the style as 'eighteenth century vernacular' and highlights the rather unusual Classical colonnade. (Although it is noted that a covered walkway is a feature found in some almshouses and was not restricted to the Classical period). It does have some nice details, in particular, the central shaped gable with swan neck pediment over the first floor window, and door surrounds in a neo-classical style.

The nineteenth century was the last great period of almshouse building. In the early part of twentieth century, the responsibility for providing housing fell to local authorities and a period of mass council house building followed. The late 1980s saw this role relinquished as 'social housing' was transferred to housing associations. Almshouses continued to be built throughout the twentieth century but the emphasis was on the accommodation and internal facilities rather than architectural showmanship. Buildings are no longer distinctive in terms of their architecture - although, no doubt they provide occupants with modern and comfortable accommodation.

What will become of those almshouses that are redundant? **Gamlyn's Almshouses** in **Spalding**, (*pg 25*) founded in 1590 and rebuilt in 1844, are no longer used as almshouses. The building which was listed grade II in 1950, comprises three two-storey blocks arranged around an open quadrangle (with separate accommodation for male and female residents in different wings). The building is in a Gothic style, built of red brick with ashlar dressings; adornments include traceried windows, crenellated parapets and oriel windows.

Many existing almshouses have been modernised and the internal arrangements altered to provide improved accommodation for occupants (and the number of units reduced as a consequence). **Snowden's Hospital** in **Scotgate, Stamford** dates from 1822 and replaced an earlier almshouse building on the same site. The building, which is in the Tudor style cost £450 to construct, and originally housed 8 widows in single rooms; each occupant had one bed-sitting room with fireplace and a shared lobby; *the plan on pg 70 shows the layout of the building*. The accommodation was later reorganised and the number of dwellings reduced to three. However, the Trustees have been unable to find anyone to occupy the properties so permission was recently granted for conversion into offices.

The need to provide modern day comforts and conveniences for elderly occupants without damaging the distinctive character and appearance of these buildings can be a problem. Some almshouses have had modern UPVC windows installed. Generally, the use of plastic windows is not considered appropriate in a historic building. However, when the glazing pattern (including opening lights) closely follows that of the original windows and the same treatment is applied to the whole row or terrace, as has been done in the **Horton almshouse** at **Frieston Road Boston**, and **The Low Nests and High Nests** in **Billingborough** (*pg 52*) then the uniformity, which is an important part of the character of almshouse buildings, is retained. Other almshouses, such as **St Anne's Bedehouses, Lincoln,** have been successfully upgraded without affecting their appearance or special interest and continue to provide comfortable accommodation with up-to-date facilities in an attractive setting.

Lincolnshire has a long history of almshouse building which continues into the twenty first century. The town of Spalding is particular notable for its almshouse provision. The proposed **Wyegate Park** development by Broadgate builders on behalf of the Spalding Town Husbands, replicates the traditional open quadrangle layout, with ten single-storey dwellings overlooking a central landscaped square. The development at **Hoekman Way,** *(pg 65)* by the same builder, is less cohesive, with the feeling of a modern housing estate, although the canopy over the front door, bay window and gable feature add visual interest.

Although almshouses were intended as a means of alleviating the plight of the poorest in society, the buildings were also a permanent monument to the generosity of the benefactor and the creation of an architectural statement often took precedence over the convenience of the occupants. The buildings were usually individually designed, often by well-known architects, and built of high quality materials. Although building styles tended to follow the fashions of the time, almshouses were built to symbolise their purpose and 'stood apart' from other cottages – this is what makes them so distinctive.

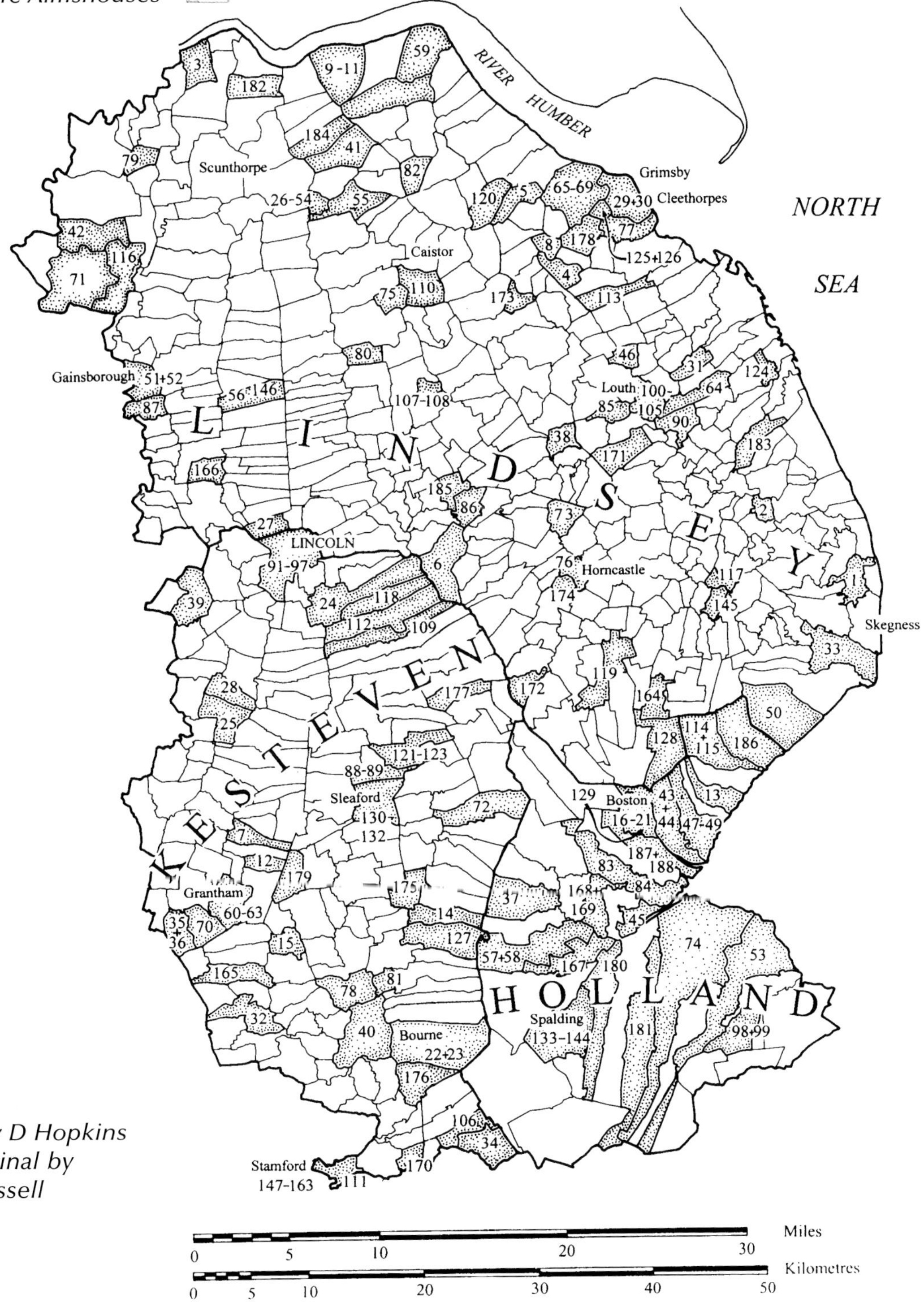

Drawn by D Hopkins from original by Rex C Russell

Medieval Hospitals and Almshouses in Lincolnshire

(see key at end of table)

No. on Map	Placename	District	Founded	Gazetteer No.	Status
1	Addlethorpe	L	1710	49	P
2	Alford	L	1668	50	S
3	Alkborough	L	before 1837	115	P
4	Ashby cum Fenby	L	before 1640	51	S
5	Aylesby	L	1925	116	S
6	Bardney	L	1708	52	S
7	Barkston	K	1640	53	S
8	Barnoldby-le-Beck	L	1968	117	S
9	Barton on Humber: Chantry House	L	1701	55	X
10	Barton on Humber: Holland's	L	1669	54	X
11	Barton on Humber: St Leonard's	L	1259	1	X
12	Belton	K	1659	56	S
13	Benington	H	1728	57	S
14	Billingborough	K	1914	118	S
15	Boothby Pagnell	K	end of 12th C	2	X
16	Boston: Horton	H	1909	120	S
17	Boston: Muster Roll Hses	H	1846	119	S
18	Boston: St John Baptist	H	pre 1282	3	X
19	Boston: St John's Row	H	pre 1685	58	X
20	Boston: St Leonard's	H	1765	59	X
21	Boston: Willoughby Road	H	1869	121	S
22	Bourne: Fisher's Almshouses	K	1620	60	X
23	Bourne: Trollope's Almshouses	K	1636	61	S
24	Branston	K	1553	62	X
25	Brant Broughton	K	1860	122	S
26	Brigg	L	1422	4	X
27	Burton by Lincoln	L	1712	63	P

28	Carlton le Moorland	K	pre 1301	5	X
29	Cleethorpes: Coronation Houses	L	1911	124	S
30	Cleethorpes : Cottage Homes	L	1902	123	S
31	Cockerington St Mary	L	1670	64	P
32	Colsterworth	K	1861	125	P
33	Croft	L	1585	65	X
34	Deeping St James	K	1956	126	S
35	Denton near Grantham: Blyth Cottages Charity	K	1696	67	S
36	Denton near Grantham: William Welby foundation	K	1786	66	X
37	Donington in Holland	H	1726	68	X
38	Donington on Bain	L	1981	127	S
39	Eagle	K	pre 1154	6	X
40	Edenham	K	pre 1319	7	X
41	Elsham	L	pre 1166	8	X
42	Epworth	L	not known	128	X
43	Fishtoft: Coronation Cotts	H	1911	130	P
44	Fishtoft	H	1828	129	X
45	Fosdyke: Middlecott's Hospital	H	1625	69	P
46	Fotherby	L	1866	131	S
47	Freiston: Clarke's	H	1595/1926	71	S
48	Freiston: Holland's	H	1604	72	X
49	Freiston: Truesdale's	H	1694	70	X
50	Friskney	L	19th & 20th C	132	S
51	Gainsborough: Frow	L	1926	133	S
52	Gainsborough: Unknown dedication	L	1495	9	X
53	Gedney	H	pre 1339	10	X
54	Glandford Bridge: (Brigg) St John Baptist	L	1422	12	X
55	Glanford Brigg: (Wrawby)	L	end of 12th C	11	X
56	Glentworth	L	1589	73	P
57	Gosberton: Church St	H	1750	75	X
58	Gosberton: Widow's Row	H	1707	74	X
59	Goxhill	L	pre 1837	134	X
60	Grantham: Hurst	K	1671	76	X
61	Grantham: Bradley's	K	1874	135	S
62	Grantham: Dawson's	K	1862	136	S
63	Grantham: St Margaret	K	pre 1328	133	X
64	Grimoldby	L	1780	77	X
65	Grimsby: Fishermen	L	1896	137	S
66	Grimsby: Flottergate	L	1933	138	S
67	Grimsby: Smedley's	L	1902	139	S
68	Grimsby: SS Mary Magdalen & Leger	L	13th C	14	X
69	Grimsby: St John's	L	pre 1389	15	X
70	Harlaxton	K	c 1820	140	P
71	Haxey	L	1723	78	X
72	Heckington	K	1886	141	S
73	Hemingby	L	1727	79	S
74	Holbeach	H	1389	16	X
75	Holton le Moor	L	1910	142	S
76	Horncastle	L	1861	143	S
77	Humberstone	L	1709	80	S
78	Irnham	K	1712	81	S
79	Keadby (near Crowle)	L	pre 1837	44	X
80	Kingerby	L	1675	82	S
81	Kirkby Underwood	K	1638	83	X
82	Kirmington	L	1888	145	P
83	Kirton in Holland: Robert Hunt's Charity	H	1663	84	S
84	Kirton in Holland: John Speak Cottage Homes	H	1928	146	S
85	Langton by Horncastle	L	1690	85	S
86	Langworth	L	pre 1313	17	X
87	Lea	L	1916	147	S
88	Leasingham: Bishop of Nottingham's	K	1885	148	S
89	Leasingham: Walter Wright's	K	1967	149	S
90	Legbourne	L	1924	150	S
91	Lincoln: Holy Innocents	K	early 12th C	18	X
97	Lincoln: St Anne's	K	1847	151	S
92	Lincoln: St Bartholomew	K	1314-1331	23	X
93	Lincoln: St Giles	K	13th C	20	X
94	Lincoln St Leonard	K	13th C	21	X
95	Lincoln: St Mary Magdalene	K	pre 1311	22	X
96	Lincoln: St Sepulchre	K	1094-1123	19	X
98	Long Sutton: Gee's	H	1913	152	X
99	Long Sutton: Winfrey's	H	1925	152	S
100	Louth: dedication unknown	L	pre 1314	24	X
101	Louth: Ayscough Trust	L	1984	155	S
102	Louth: Edward VI	L	1551	86	S
103	Louth: Orme	L	1885	154	S
104	Louth: St Mary	L	16th C	26	X
105	Louth: Trinity	L	16th C	25	X
106	Market Deeping	K	1876	156	S
107	Market Rasen: St Poll Hospital	L	1612	87	S
108	Market Rasen: Young's	L	1832	157	P
109	Mere (Dunston psh):	K	13th C	27	X
110	Nettleton	L	c 1920	158	S
111	Newstead	K	pre 1200	28	X
112	Nocton	K	19th C	159	P
113	North Thoresby	L	1935	160	S
114	Old Leake: Alenson & Erskine	H	pre 1939	162	S
115	Old Leake: Harlock	H	20th C	161	S
116	Owston Ferry	L	1860	163	S
117	Partney	L	after 1115	29	X
118	Potterhanworth	K	1776	88	X
119	Revesby	L	1726	89	S
120	Riby	L	1848	164	X
121	Ruskington: Teetotal Houses	K	1887	165	S
122	Ruskington: Hodgson House	K	1719	90	X
123	Ruskington: Scott's	K	1904	166	S
124	Saltfleetby: All Saints	L	1785	91	X
125	Scartho	L	c 1930	168	S
126	Scartho	L	2000	167	S
127	Sempringham	K	n.d.	30	X
128	Sibsey	L	20th C	169	S
129	Skirbeck	H	pre 1230	31	X
130	Sleaford: Carres	K	1636	92	S
131	Sleaford: Jessie Snow's	K	1952	170	S
132	Sleaford: Hussey	K	1538	32	X
133	Spalding: Dalton Homes	H	1938	172	S
134	Spalding: Gamlyn's	H	1650	93	P
135	Spalding: Kingston Cottage Homes	H	1907	171	S
136	Spalding: Galls	H	1971	173	S
137	Spalding: Lot Mael's	H	1708	96	X
138	Spalding: Masham	H	1960	174	S
139	Spalding: Mrs E Sparke's	H	1717	94	X
140	Spalding: St Nicholas	H	pre 1323	33	X

141	Spalding: Van Geest	H	1994	175	S
142	Spalding: Warrell	H	1697	95	X
143	Spalding: Wm Willsby's	H	1592	97	X
144	Spalding; Alice Wilson	H	1981	176	S
145	Spilsby	L	1949	177	S
146	Spital in the Street	L	1396	34	P
147	Stamford: Fryer's Callis	K	1832	178	S
148	Stamford: Truesdale	K	1700	99	S
149	Stamford: Hopkin's	K	1770	101	S
150	Stamford: Williamson's	K	1770	103	P
151	Stamford: All Saints (now Brown's)	K	1485	41	S
152	Stamford: Domus Dei	K	pre 1414	42	X
153	Stamford: Burghley's	K	1597	102	S
154	Stamford: All Saints Callis	K	pre 1800	100	X
155	Stamford: Snowdens	K	1604	98	P
156	Stamford: St Giles Hosp	K	13th C	38	X
157	Stamford: St Giles outside	K	pre 1304	40	X
158	Stamford: St Helen's	K	pre 1547	43	X
159	Not allocated				
160	Stamford: St John and St Thomas	K	pre 1323	37	X
161	Stamford: St Leger	K	pre 1199	35	X
162	Stamford: St Peter's	K	pre 1466	44	X
163	Stamford: St Sepulchre	K	pre 1189	36	X
164	Stickney	L	1600	104	S
165	Stoke Rochford	K	1677	105	S
166	Sturton by Stow	L	pre 1837	179	X
167	Surfleet	H	1912	180	S
168	Sutterton: Claydam	H	1567	107	X
169	Sutterton	H	c 1592	106	X
170	Tallington	K	1582	108	S
171	Tathwell	L	c 1972	181	S
172	Tattershall	L	1440	45	S
173	Thorganby	L	1966	182	S
174	Thornton	L	pre 1530	46	X
175	Threekingham	K	pre 1319	47	X
176	Thurlby	K	1953	183	S
177	Walcot	K	pre 1311	48	X
178	Waltham	L	1938	184	S
179	Welby	K	1780	109	X
180	Weston	H	1969	185	S
181	Whaplode	H	1624	110	S
182	Winterton	L	1907	186	S
183	Withern	L	1907	187	S
184	Worlaby	L	1663	111	P
185	Wragby	L	1697	112	S
186	Wrangle	H	1555	113	S
187	Wyberton: Field, Anderson and Tooley	H	1624	114	S
188	Wyberton: Cooke-Yarborough	H	1965	188	S

Key:

Status:
- **X** Building no longer exists
- **S** Still in use as an almshouse (but may be a rebuilding of original)
- **P** Building survives, but not now in use as an almshouse

District:
- **H** Holland
- **K** Kesteven
- **L** Lindsey

Further Reading

Bailey B — *Almshouses*, Robert Hale, London,1988

Blore T — *Stanford Charities* [sic], Drakard, Stamford, 1813

Duffy E — *The Stripping of the Altars*, Yale, 1992

Fowler Revd J — *Richard Waldo Sibthorp: A Biography*, W Skeffington & Don, 1880

Godfrey W H — *The English Almshouse*, Faber & Faber, 1955

Goodall J A A — *God's House at Ewelme*, Ashgate Publishing Ltd. Aldershot, 2001

Hartley J S and Roger A — *The Religious Foundations of Medieval Stamford*; Department of Education, University of Nottingham, 1974

Hill Sir F — *Tudor and Stuart Lincoln*, Cambridge University Press, 1956

Hill Sir F — *Medieval Lincoln*, Cambridge University Press, 1965

Howson B — *Houses of Noble Poverty*, Bellevue Books Sunbury-on-Thames, 1993

Knowles D & Hadcock R N — *Medieval Religious Houses, England and Wales*, Longmans, Green & Co. London, 1953

Owen D — *Church and Society in Medieval Lincolnshire*, History of Lincolnshire Volume V, History of Lincolnshire Committee, Lincoln, 1981

Page W (ed) — *Victoria County History of Lincolnshire Volume II*, London, 1906

Pevsner N & Harris J — *The Buildings of England – Lincolnshire*, Penguin, London, (2nd ed revised by Antram N), 1990

Prescott E — *The English Medieval Hospital*, Seaby, 1992

Rawcliffe C — *Medicine for the Soul*, Alan Sutton, 1999

Thompson P — *The History and Antiquities of Boston and the Hundred of Skirbeck*, 1856 reprinted edition 1997, Heritage Lincolnshire, Sleaford

Woodfield C & Woodfield P — *Lyddington Bede House, English Heritage*, London, 1988 (reprinted 1999)

Notes to Chapters

1100-1550 Medieval Hospitals

1 English Heritage, August 1989, Monuments Protection Programme, Monument Class Description, Hospitals

2 Franklin, M J, 1986, The Beginnings of Newstead-by-Stamford Priory in *Lincolnshire History & Archaeology*, Vol 21, pp35-37

3 Lincolnshire Archives Office: Register XXVI ff 122v-123r

4 Boulter, S, 1992, *Death and Disease in Medieval Grantham,* unpublished dissertation for BSc (hons) degree, University of Sheffield

5 Hill, Sir Francis, 1956, *Tudor and Stuart Lincoln*, p67, Cambridge University Press

6 Lincolnshire Archives Office: LD40/45 BRA328

7 Knowles, D & Hadcock, R N, 1953, *Medieval Religious Houses, England and Wales*, p235. Longmans, Green & Co. London

8 Brooks, F W, 1937, The Hospital of the Holy Innocents without Lincoln, in *Reports & Papers of the Architectural and Archaeological Societies of the Counties of Lincoln & Northampton*, Vol XLII, Part II, pp157-188

9 Steane, K *et al.*, forthcoming, *The Archaeology of the Upper City*, Lincoln Archaeological Studies Vol 3, Oxbow Books, Oxford

10 Codicum Manuscriptorum, vol xxxix p422, Lincoln Diocese no. 17, per Dominum Edmund Lake Domini Episcopi Lincoln Cancellarium

11 Stocker, D, 1993 The Early Church in Lincolnshire in *Pre-Viking Lindsey* (ed. Vince, A.) p110; Lincoln Archaeological Studies: No 1, City of Lincoln Archaeological Unit, Lincoln

12 PRO E315/393

13 Liber cantariarum p399

14 Hartley, J S and Roger, A, 1974, *The Religious Foundations of Medieval Stamford,* Department of Education, University of Nottingham

15 Lincolnshire Archives Office: 77 G136.7

16 Thornton College Almshouses, *Lincolnshire Notes and Queries* Vol. XVIII p29

1550-1800 The Evolution of the Almshouse

1 Trollope, Anthony, 1855, *The Warden*, reprinted (8th impression) in World Classics, Oxford University Press

2 Hill, Sir Francis, 1956, *Tudor and Stuart Lincoln*, p138, Cambridge University Press

3 Lincolnshire Archives Office: MCD 171 ANC V/D/22 letter dated 27 September 1937 to Mrs Rudkin from H Holderman

4 Lincolnshire Archives Office: Wrangle par 15/4

5 Lincolnshire Archives Office: LCC Admon 1669/181

6 Lincolnshire Archives Office: LCC Admon 1669/181

7 Lincolnshire Archives Office: V/D/22/ANC letter a

8 Lincolnshire Archives Office: Dec 1752 V/D/22 ANC letter h

9 Lincolnshire Archives Office: V/D/22 ANC letter c

10 Lincolnshire Archives Office: 1851 HO 107 2094/49

1800-2000 From Picturesque to Plain

No Notes

A Legacy of Almshouse Building

1 Smith, M, 2000, *The Story of Stamford*, p118, Smith/Walker's Books Ltd, Stamford

General Sources

Charity Commissioners' Report, 1837, published in 1990

Census Returns

Kelly's Directory (1905 and 1933)

Whites Directory (1856 and 1872)

Wright, Joseph, 1898, *Dialect Dictionary*, first published 1898, reprinted 1970 Fletcher and son Ltd., Norwich

Index

Figures in **bold** indicate a gazetteer entry
Figures in *italics* indicate an illustration caption